Independent Schools
Examinations Board

SCIENCE PRACTICE EXERCISES
13+

Ron Pickering

Independent Schools
Examinations Board

www.galorepark.co.uk

GALORE PARK

Published by Galore Park Publishing Ltd
Carmelite House, 50 Victoria Embankment, London EC4Y 0DZ
www.galorepark.co.uk

Design and typography Typetechnique

Printed and bound by CPI Group (UK) Ltd, Croydon, CR0 4YY

ISBN: 978 1 907047 23 7

First published 2010, reprinted 2011, 2012, 2014, 2015

Details of other ISEB publications and examination papers, and Galore Park
publications are available at www.galorepark.co.uk

6

Contents

Introduction

Science Practice Exercises 13+ is a book of sample exercises in the Common Entrance style, based on the ISEB syllabus for Science.

Unlike a Common Entrance exam paper, each chapter of the book tests a single topic. The aim of this structure is to allow you to focus on the topics in which you feel you are weakest, reinforcing your understanding of key terms, as well as your knowledge of the relevant natural forces and processes.

Just as in the Common Entrance papers, each test begins with a series of multiple choice questions. These questions will very quickly tell you whether you know the basics of the test topic.

Exam paper structure

At 13+, the Common Entrance Science exam is divided into three papers: one for Life Processes and Living Things (Biology), one for Materials and their Properties (Chemistry), and one for Physical Processes (Physics).

Be aware, when you start your exam that you will be tested on several topics in the same paper.

Timing

Try to complete each test within 40 minutes, which is the time allocated to each exam paper.

If you are entitled to extra time, use it as you have been advised by your teacher.

Drawing graphs

You should write all of your answers on separate paper (not in the book), and this includes drawing graphs. Where a graph is provided in the book, copy it (including axes, numbers and labels) on to graph paper and draw points and lines as required.

A collection of all the graphs in this book is available as a download from the Galore Park website www.galorepark.co.uk.

I wish you the best of luck with these test exercises and, of course, with the 'real thing'.

Ron Pickering
2010

Biology

1: Cells and organisation

1.1 Which option best completes each of the following sentences? (10)

(a) Respiration is

producing offspring	releasing energy
taking in nutrients	responding to stimuli

(b) Excretion is

taking in nutrients	getting rid of poisonous wastes
releasing energy	increasing in size

(c) The human male gamete is a

liver cell	pollen grain
sperm cell	nerve cell

(d) Reproduction is

producing offspring	releasing energy
taking in nutrients	increasing in size

(e) Nutrition is

producing offspring	releasing energy
taking in nutrients	responding to stimuli

(f) The basic unit of life is

a molecule	an organ
a tissue	a cell

(g) The function of goblet cells in the human trachea is to

sweep away particles of dust	release waste carbon dioxide
secrete mucus	absorb oxygen for respiration

(h) A collection of cells with the same function is

an organism	an organ
a tissue	a system

(i) A cell with a nucleus, cell wall and a large surface area for absorption is a

red blood cell	nerve cell
leaf cell	root hair cell

(j) A cell that has the power of contraction is a

liver cell	white blood cell
nerve cell	muscle cell

1.2 The diagram shows a single celled organism called *Chlamydomonas*. This organism is able to swim about in the small puddles of water where it lives.

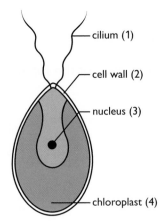

cilium (1)

cell wall (2)

nucleus (3)

chloroplast (4)

(a) In this table, which set of numbers (A, B, C or D) correctly relates functions of cell parts to the structures labelled in the diagram? (2)

	function			
	protection against bursting	**photosynthesis**	**movement**	**control of cell activities**
A	2	4	1	3
B	1	3	2	4
C	4	2	1	3
D	2	4	3	1

(b) Name **three** structures in the *Chlamydomonas* cell which would not be found in a sperm cell. (3)

1.3 The diagrams below show six cells.

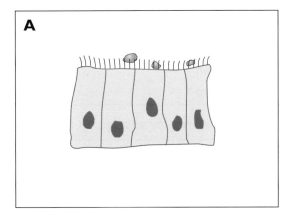

A

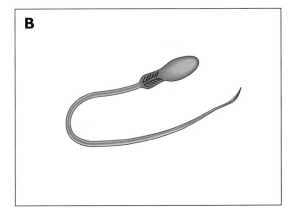

B

2

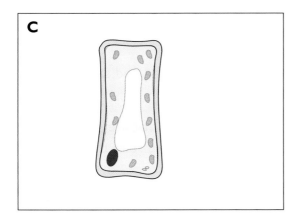

C

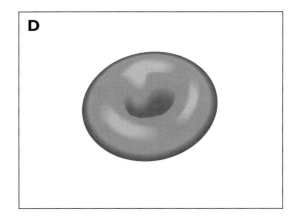

D

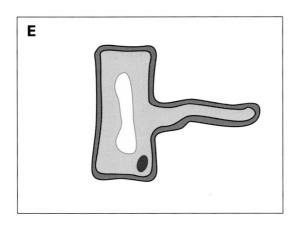

E

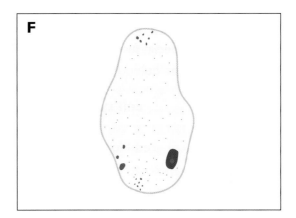

F

(a) (i)   Give the letter of the ciliated cell.   (1)
    (ii) What is the function of cilia?   (1)

(b) Give the letter of the cell that carries genetic information from father
    to offspring.   (1)

(c) Give the letters of **two** plant cells.   (2)

(d) Give the letter of the cell with a surface adapted for the uptake of minerals.   (1)

1.4 (a) The diagram below shows a plant cell and an animal cell.

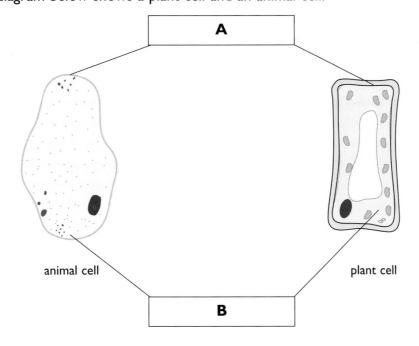

A

animal cell   plant cell

B

(i) Give the names of **two** parts that are present in plant cells but not in animal cells. (2)

(ii) Give the function of **one** of the parts you have named, and say why it is important in the life of the plant. (2)

(iii) The letters, A and B, and guidelines show two parts that are present in both plant and animal cells. Identify the two parts, and state the function of each of them. (4)

(b) (i) Cells can become **specialised**. What does this word mean? (1)

(ii) Tissues carry out their functions because of the specialised cells they contain. Copy the words in the boxes below and then link together the cells, their special functions and the biological process they are involved in. The first cell has been done as an example. (4)

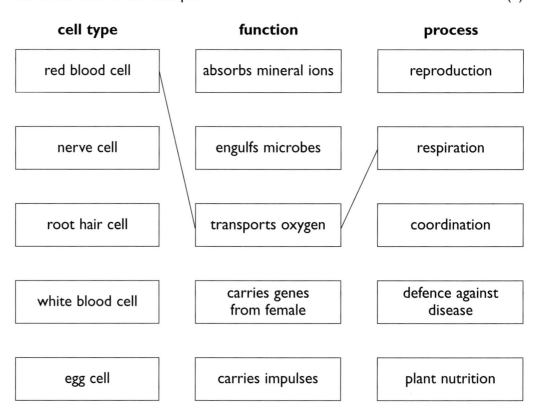

cell type	function	process
red blood cell	absorbs mineral ions	reproduction
nerve cell	engulfs microbes	respiration
root hair cell	transports oxygen	coordination
white blood cell	carries genes from female	defence against disease
egg cell	carries impulses	plant nutrition

1.5 The diagram shows a plant cell.

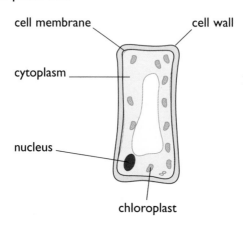

cell membrane   cell wall

cytoplasm

nucleus

chloroplast

(a) (i) This cell is from the leaf of a sycamore tree. Name the part which is present in this cell but would not be present in a root cell from a sycamore tree. (1)

   (ii) Why is the part you have chosen in part (i), not present in a root cell? (1)

(b) The parts labelled in this diagram have different functions. Copy and complete the table below to link each part to its correct function. (5)

part of cell	function
	helps keep cell shape
	controls the entry and exit of substances
	contains the genetic material that controls the cell's activities
	many chemical reactions take place here
	the site of the trapping of light for photosynthesis

1.6 The human body contains several different systems. The systems are made up of organs working together so that the body is at its most efficient.

This is a list of some of the organs of the human body. Copy and complete the table below to match the organs to the system they belong to. (9)

teeth	rib	stomach
heart	testes	lungs
bladder	brain	biceps

system	organs in this system
digestive	
circulatory	
excretory	
reproductive	
nervous	
breathing	
skeletal	

2: Nutrition and health

2.1 Which option best completes each of the following sentences? (10)

(a) The most important food for muscle growth and repair is

fat	calcium
carbohydrate	protein

(b) A molecule which speeds up digestion but remains unchanged itself is

a protein	a mineral
an enzyme	a vitamin

(c) Cabbage is a good source of

fat	sugar
vitamin D	fibre

(d) Digested protein enters the blood in the

stomach	small intestine
liver	kidney

(e) Iodine solution is a stain used to detect

protein	fat
sugar	starch

(f) Calcium is essential in a balanced diet to

prevent scurvy	supply energy
help develop strong bones	help digestion

(g) The use of different foods in the body is the process of

digestion	absorption
assimilation	respiration

(h) Red blood cells only develop properly if the diet contains plenty of

starch	calcium
vitamin C	iron

(i) Egg whites are a good source of

sugar	fat
protein	starch

(j) The most important teeth for biting off pieces of an apple are the

molars	pre-molars
canines	incisors

2.2 The table below provides information about five different foods.

food	energy content (kJ per 100 g)	nutrients (per 100 g)			
		carbohydrate (g)	fat (g)	protein (g)	calcium (mg)
yoghurt	280	5.0	4.0	3.0	120
cheese	1700	0.2	35.2	24.0	710
pear	380	26.1	0.1	0.8	6
brown rice	900	42.7	1.8	9.5	64
butter	3118	0	82.1	0.4	17

(a) (i) Which of the nutrients provides most of the energy in the brown rice? (1)

(ii) Which of the four nutrients provides insulation against cold? (1)

(iii) Which of the foods would be most useful to a weightlifter needing to build his muscles? (1)

(b) (i) What is the total amount of the three nutrients, fat, protein and carbohydrate, in yoghurt? (1)

(ii) What makes up most of the rest of the 100 g of yoghurt? (1)

(c) (i) A teenage boy needs about 9000 kJ of energy every day. How much brown rice would he need to eat to obtain this amount of energy? (1)

(ii) The boy also needs about 55 g of protein every day. Would this same amount of rice provide all of his protein requirements? (1)

(d) The table below shows the recommended daily amount (RDA) of calcium for a female at different times in her life.

stage of life cycle	RDA of calcium (mg)
baby aged 3 months	450
12-year-old girl	900
21-year-old, non-pregnant woman	550
pregnant woman	1200
breast-feeding woman	

(i) Suggest what would be the RDA for a breast-feeding woman.

Explain your answer. (1)

(ii) Explain why the 12-year-old girl has a higher RDA of calcium than the 21-year-old woman. (1)

(iii) The 21-year-old woman needs twice as much iron as the 12-year-old girl.

Why do we need iron in our diet? (1)

2.3 This diagram shows the digestive system in a human.

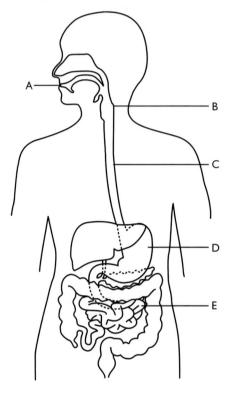

(a) (i) Which letter labels the part where there are the most villi? (1)

(ii) Which letter labels the part where the juices are acidic and start to digest protein? (1)

(iii) Proteins are digested to amino acids. How are the amino acids carried to other parts of the body? (1)

(b) A protein-digesting enzyme can be obtained from bacterial cells. This enzyme can be used to investigate the effect of temperature on the digestion of protein in milk.

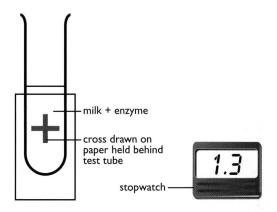

milk + enzyme

cross drawn on paper held behind test tube

stopwatch

The time recorded is the time taken for the enzyme to remove the protein and make the milk go clear. This means the cross on the paper can be seen through the clear solution.

One investigation like this gave the following results.

temperature (°C)	time taken to digest milk protein (minutes)
15	11.5
25	7.0
35	2.5
45	3.5
55	6.5
65	18.0

(i)   Plot these results on a graph grid like the one on the next page.   (4)

(ii) Give a suitable title for the graph.   (1)

(iii) What is the average human body temperature?   (1)

(iv) How does your answer to part (iii) fit in with the results you have plotted on this graph?   (1)

(v) Give **two** factors which should be kept constant if this is to be a fair test.   (2)

9

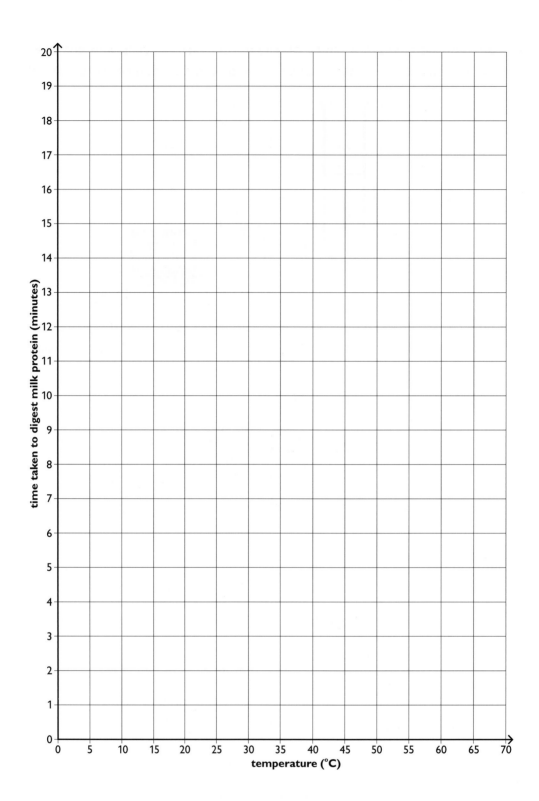

2.4 (a) Poor diet can lead to bad health. Copy the words in the boxes below and then draw lines to match up each fact about the diet to the harm it may cause. (3)

fact about diet

| too much salt |
| too little iron |
| too much fat |
| not enough fibre |
| too little protein |

harm caused

| constipation |
| high blood pressure |
| slow growth of muscles |
| cannot carry enough oxygen in blood |
| heart disease |

(b) A properly balanced diet should help to prevent this harm. Copy the words in the boxes below and then link each of these components of a balanced diet to its function in a healthy body. (3)

component of diet

| sugar |
| calcium |
| vitamin C |
| water |
| starch |

function in a healthy body

| required for development of bones and teeth |
| an important part of the process of digesting foods |
| the main source of energy for working cells |
| provides a slow, steady supply of sugar |
| prevents scurvy |

2.5 Sally investigated the pH of milk left in a sealed container for five days. She obtained the following results:

time (days)	pH of sealed milk sample
0	7.1
1	6.4
2	5.9
3	5.2
4	4.5
5	4.1

(i) Plot these results on a graph grid like the one below. (3)

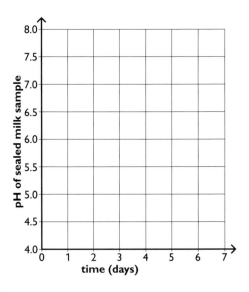

(ii) Sally believed that bacteria were causing this change in pH. What were the bacteria releasing to bring about this change? (1)

(iii) Use the graph to predict the likely pH after 7 days. (1)

(iv) Sally decided to try to find out if heating the milk would stop this pH change. Describe in detail how she could do this. Use the terms **independent variable**, **dependent variable** and **controlled variable** in your answer. (4)

(v) Humans use this information on the effect of bacteria on milk in many ways. Name **one** food which humans use which is made by letting bacteria turn milk sour. (1)

(vi) If we wish to prevent milk from going sour there are many things that we can do to it. Choose **two** treatments from this list which would help to prevent milk from going sour. (1)

keep the milk at a low temperature in a refrigerator
mix the milk with fruit juice
dry the milk and store it as granules
always shake the milk before pouring it

For **one** of your choices, explain why the treatment will stop the milk from going sour. (1)

3: Reproduction

3.1 Which option best completes each of the following sentences? (10)

(a) The human male gamete is

| an ovum | an antibody |
| a sperm | a zygote |

(b) A young woman ovulates every

| three weeks | 28 days |
| 28 weeks | three months |

(c) The process when gametes join together is called

| ovulation | gestation |
| menstruation | fertilisation |

(d) Sperm are produced in the

| sperm duct | testis |
| scrotum | penis |

(e) The genes from the two parents are carried in the part of the sex cell called the

| cytoplasm | membrane |
| nucleus | embryo |

(f) The stage of human development at which a person becomes able to reproduce is called

| adulthood | gestation |
| activity | puberty |

(g) Two sex cells join together to form

| an embryo | a zygote |
| a fetus | a gamete |

(h) The part of the body where substances can be exchanged between a pregnant woman and her developing baby is the

| liver | umbilical cord |
| placenta | amniotic sac |

(i) Growth and development are controlled by chemicals called

| vitamins | haemoglobin |
| minerals | hormones |

(j) The length of time between fertilisation and birth is called

| gestation | conception |
| menstruation | copulation |

3.2 The diagram below shows the reproductive system of a male.

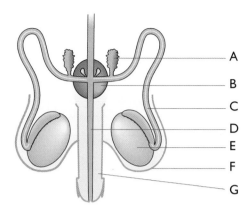

(a) Which of the labelled structures (choose the correct letter in each case)

   (i) produces sperm? (1)

   (ii) carries urine as well as sperm? (1)

   (iii) produces a fluid for sperm to swim in? (1)

(b) (i) Which structure, shown in the diagram, is cut in a common contraceptive operation? (1)

   (ii) Explain why this operation is a successful form of contraception. (1)

(c) A chemical called testosterone is produced in a boy's body from adolescence onwards. This chemical causes certain changes in the boy's body.

   (i) Where is this chemical produced? (1)

   (ii) Describe **two** changes caused by testosterone. (2)

3.3 During pregnancy a woman's body undergoes many changes. One noticeable change is that her body swells as the fetus grows. This table shows the changes in mass of some of her body parts. Answer the questions on the next page.

body part	increase in mass (kg)
uterus	1.0
breast tissue	0.4
fat	3.7
placenta	0.7
blood	0.4
amniotic fluid	0.8

(a) (i) Use the figures in the table on page 15 to plot a bar chart on a grid like the one below. Do **not** include the figure for fat in your bar chart. (3)

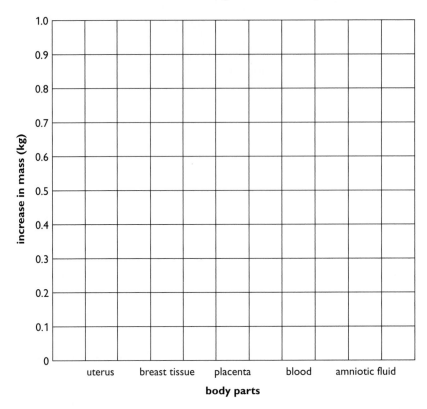

(ii) The mother also gains about 1.5 kg of water and about 0.5 kg of bone. Calculate the total gain in mass, including the figure for fat, during pregnancy. (1)

(iii) What proportion of this gain in mass is due to the placenta? Show your working. (2)

(b) Explain why the pregnant woman must make sure that she has plenty of **iron** and **calcium** in her diet. (2)

(c) Mothers who smoke during pregnancy risk harming their babies. Tobacco smoke contains many chemicals, including **nicotine** and **carbon monoxide gas** (this gas combines with red blood cells). Explain how these might cause damage to the developing fetus. (2)

3.4 The diagrams below show some cells.

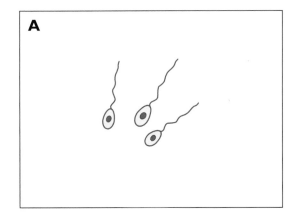

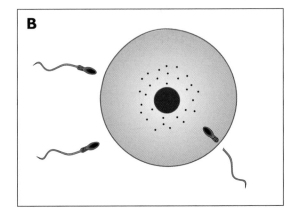

16

(a) (i) What is the name of cell A? (1)

   (ii) Give **two** ways in which this cell is adapted to its function. (2)

(b) (i) What process is shown in B? (1)

   (ii) Where does this process take place? (1)

(c) Copy and complete the following sentences. (4)

About six days after process B occurs a ball of cells called an . . . . becomes embedded in the thickened wall of the . . . . This process is called . . . . , and once it has successfully been completed a new structure called the . . . . forms, linking the mother to her developing baby.

3.5 This question is about the menstrual cycle.

(a) Copy and complete the following sentences. (5)

One of the . . . . releases an egg cell (ovum) every . . . . If there is no fertilisation, or the fertilised egg does not stick to the lining of the womb, then . . . . occurs. When this process occurs, a woman loses . . . . – this is often called 'having a . . . .'.

(b) This diagram shows the lining of the uterus during the menstrual cycle.

Day 1   Day 4   Day 10   Day 14   Day 17   Day 28

Between or around which days is the time

(i) of ovulation? (1)

(ii) when the uterus lining is lost? (1)

(iii) when fertilisation is most likely? (1)

3.6 This diagram shows a fetus in the uterus just before birth.

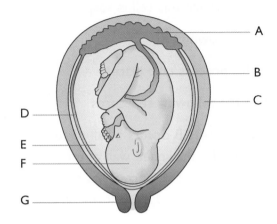

(a) Which letter labels

    (i)   the amniotic sac? (1)

    (ii) the umbilical cord? (1)

    (iii) a muscle which can push out the baby at birth? (1)

(b) What is the function of the amniotic fluid around the fetus? (1)

(c) The pregnant woman sometimes has cravings for particular foods. Many women like to have milk chocolate, which contains a lot of sugar. Explain in detail how this sugar reaches the developing fetus while the fetus is inside its mother's uterus? (4)

(d) What is the normal length of pregnancy in humans in months? (1)

4: Respiration, energy and exercise

4.1 Which option best completes each of the following sentences? (10)

(a) The ends of bones are protected by

ligament	muscle
tendon	cartilage

(b) Gas exchange in humans takes place in the

trachea	alveoli
villi	bronchi

(c) A gas which turns limewater milky is

oxygen	carbon monoxide
carbon dioxide	water vapour

(d) In the blood oxygen is transported in the

plasma	platelets
white blood cells	red blood cells

(e) Cigarette smoking does not cause harm to the

lungs	heart
fingernails	unborn baby

(f) The release of energy by the oxidation of food is

digestion	excretion
absorption	respiration

(g) When cigarette smoke is bubbled through Universal Indicator solution, the solution changes from

red to yellow	green to red/orange
blue to green	green to blue

(h) The tissue which joins muscle to bone is

tendon	cartilage
ligament	epidermis

(i) Muscles which help in breathing are

biceps and triceps	diaphragm and biceps
intercostals and diaphragm	intercostals and triceps

(j) Respiration does not release

carbon dioxide	water
heat	glucose

4.2 The diagram shows the rib cage in a human.

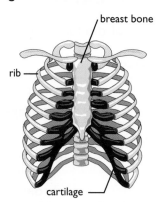

(a) The rib cage is able to move during breathing.

   (i) Which type of tissue is responsible for this movement? (1)

   (ii) In which direction do the ribs move when we breathe in? (1)

(b) The rib cage also plays a part in protecting delicate organs. Give the names of **two** organs which the rib cage protects. (2)

(c) There are other sets of bones involved in movement. This diagram shows the bones of the human arm.

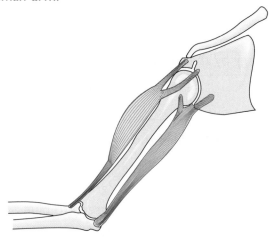

   (i) What is the muscle called that contracts to straighten the arm? (1)

   (ii) What is the muscle called that contracts to bend the arm? (1)

   (iii) The muscles make up a pair. One of them relaxes while the other one is contracting. What is the scientific name for this kind of pairing? (1)

(d) (i) The ends of the bones in the elbow joint are covered by cartilage, and there is a fluid in a sac around the joint. Why are the cartilage and the fluid important? (1)

   (ii) Sometimes the cartilage becomes worn and small pieces break off. What is the name of this disease? (1)

4.3 Anika is a good athlete, and wanted to find out how training was affecting her breathing. She was able to use a machine which measures the volume of air breathed in and out – the machine allows measurements to be made **before** and **during** exercise.

(a) The chart shows results obtained during one investigation.

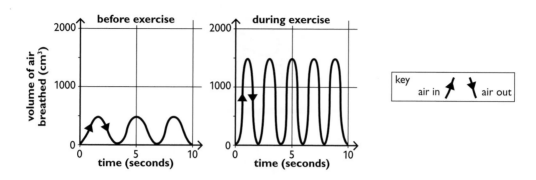

(i) How much more air did Anika breathe in with each breath during exercise (in cm^3)? (1)

(ii) The air contains 20% oxygen. How much more **oxygen** did Anika breathe in per **minute**? Show your working. (4)

(iii) Copy and complete this word equation to explain why Anika breathed in this extra oxygen during the period of exercise. (2)

. . . . + oxygen → . . . . + water + ...

(b) Which other organ in Anika's body would work faster to help this extra oxygen reach the parts of the body where it is needed? (1)

(c) The diagram below shows the muscles in Anika's leg.

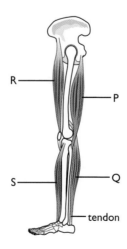

(i) Which muscle contracts when Anika stands on tip toe? (1)

(ii) Which muscle contracts as Anika lifts her leg and bends her knee as she starts to exercise? (1)

21

4.4 David wanted to compare the energy value of several foods. He used the apparatus shown below, and measured the rise in temperature caused by the burning food sample.

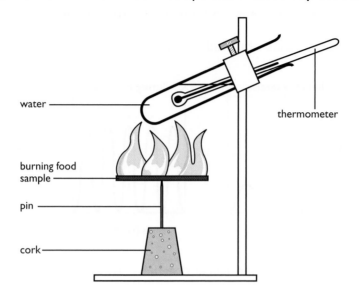

(a) (i) What is the **independent** (input) **variable** in his experiment? (1)

(ii) What is the **dependent** (outcome) **variable** in his experiment? (1)

(iii) Suggest **two** steps that David should take to make this a fair test. (2)

(iv) David's teacher suggested collecting all of the class results together before trying to draw conclusions. Why is this important? (2)

(b) (i) In a living cell the food does not burn in this way to release energy. What is the name of the process which releases energy from foods in living cells? (1)

(ii) Give **two** reasons why energy is required in the body. (2)

4.5 The diagram below shows part of a human breathing system.

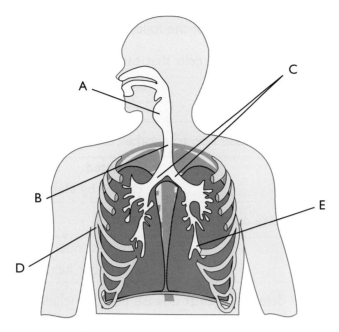

(a) Give the letters which label

(i) the part which is lined with ciliated cells (1)

(ii) the part where gases are exchanged between blood and air (1)

(b) The diagram below shows some specialised cells from the region you have identified in (a) (i).

(i) The specialised cells work together to perform one function. What is the name given to a group of specialised cells with the same function? (1)

(ii) Describe how these cells and their products help to keep the lungs free of dust and bacteria. (2)

(iii) Carbon monoxide damages the cilia, and tar irritates the cells so that they make more mucus. What will be the result of this for a cigarette smoker? (2)

(c) (i) Which gas passes from air to blood in the part you have identified in (a) (ii)? (1)

(ii) Which gas passes from blood to air? (1)

(iii) What is the name of the process which moves the particles of these gases? (1)

(iv) The lining which these gases cross is **thin** and with a **large surface area**. Explain why each of these features is important. (2)

5: Health and disease

5.1   Which option best completes each of the following sentences?   (10)

(a)   A protein made by white blood cells that can defend against microbes is

an antibiotic	an antibody
an antiseptic	a phagocyte

(b)   A disease which can be passed on to another, unrelated person is

infectious	inherited
fatal	caused by lifestyle

(c)   The benefits of exercise do not include

increased stamina	athlete's foot
greater strength	a stronger heart

(d)   The body's natural defences against disease do not include

skin	wearing gloves when handling food
blood clots	white blood cells

(e)   A bacterial cell does not have

a membrane	cytoplasm
a nucleus	a cell wall

(f)   An example of an infectious disease is

lung cancer	influenza
heart disease	depression

(g)   Excessive use of alcohol can cause

tuberculosis	AIDS
a cold	liver damage

(h)   A disease caused by a bacterium is

influenza	meningitis
athlete's foot	AIDS

(i)   A compound that can reduce the growth of bacteria inside the body is

an antiseptic	aspirin
an antibody	an antibiotic

(j)   Fibre is needed in the diet to reduce the risk of

constipation	brain tumours
liver damage	weakened bones

5.2 Doctors have studied the factors that affect heart disease in males in the United Kingdom. Some of their results are shown in this bar chart.

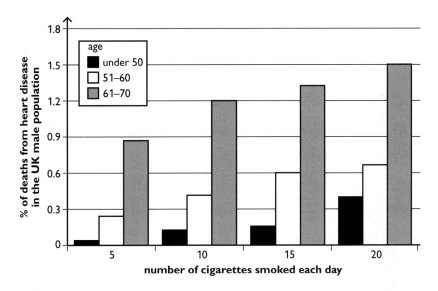

(a) Write **two** conclusions about the effect of smoking on heart disease in males. (2)

(b) This diagram shows the effect of smoking on the arteries of the heart.

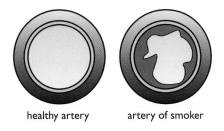

healthy artery   artery of smoker

   (i) Explain how this could cause damage to the heart. (2)

   (ii) Smoking also causes a rise in blood pressure. Explain how this could affect the health of a smoker. (1)

(c) Anna smokes every day. This graph shows the amount of nicotine in her blood after smoking a cigarette. She feels the need for a cigarette once the nicotine level falls below the 'demand threshold'. Answer the questions on the next page.

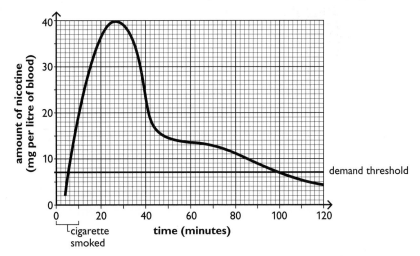

(i) How often does Anna need to smoke to keep the nicotine level above the threshold? (1)

(ii) Suggest why Anna feels anxious and bad-tempered when she wakes up in the morning. (1)

(iii) Smoking twenty cigarettes per day doubles the 'demand threshold'. Where would the new 'demand threshold' be on the graph? (1)

(iv) What effect will this have on the length of time between cigarettes that Anna can wait without becoming stressed? (1)

(v) Suggest **one** other way that Anna can satisfy her craving without smoking a cigarette. (1)

5.3 This diagram shows a simple virus.

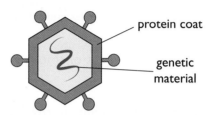

Viruses reproduce inside living cells, and often cause disease.

(a) (i) Name **one** disease caused by a virus. (1)

(ii) Diseases caused by viruses can be managed by a vaccination. Sometimes a booster injection of vaccine is needed for full protection. This diagram shows the number of antibody molecules in the blood following vaccination.

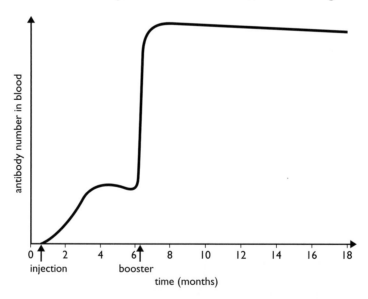

Give **three** ways in which the effect of the booster injection is different to the effect of the first injection. (3)

(b) Some viruses can change their genetic material. As a result they can alter the proteins on their coat. Explain why this makes them less likely to be controlled by the vaccine. (2)

5.4 Drinking alcohol causes changes in the way the body works.

(a) Copy the words in the boxes below and then draw lines to link the **changes** to the **effects** they have on a drinker's actions and health. (3)

change	effect on actions and health
nerve impulses travel more slowly	poor judgement of distance
blood vessels close to the skin open up	long-term liver damage
senses work less well	person looks red-faced
liver cells try to remove alcohol from blood	reactions are slowed

(b) A pregnant woman can pass any alcohol she drinks to the fetus.

(i) Describe in detail how the alcohol would reach the fetus. (3)

(ii) If the woman also smokes she may harm her unborn baby even more. How does carbon monoxide in smoke affect the health of the unborn baby? (1)

5.5 Scientists are sure that a healthy diet reduces the risk of disease. They often recommend certain foods to improve health. One of these is mycoprotein, an artificial 'meat' made from the bodies of harmless fungi.

(a) The bar chart shows the levels of different nutrients in mycoprotein and in beef.

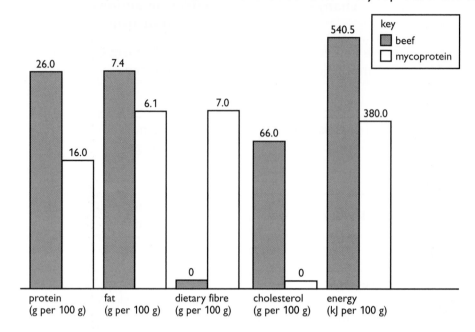

(i) Explain **three** reasons why mycoprotein is healthier than beef. (3)

(ii) Give **two** reasons why it might be better to eat beef than mycoprotein. (2)

(b) The scientists also recommend that we eat more fibre in our diet. They have compared the intake of fibre with the chance of developing colon cancer (the colon is part of the large intestine). This scatter graph shows their results.

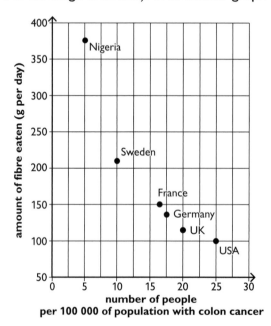

(i) Which country had the largest proportion of people with colon cancer? (1)

(ii) How much more likely is a person in the UK to have colon cancer than one from Nigeria? Explain how you reached your answer. (2)

(iii) Which **two** of the following foods are good sources of fibre? (2)

| wholemeal bread | cheese | eggs |
| chocolate | apples | pizza |

5.6 Tolani and Fumi ate some soft ice cream on school Sports Day. There were food-poisoning bacteria in the ice cream, and they became quite ill the next day. The school doctor gave them antibiotics, and told them to take them for eight days.

This graph shows the change in the number of bacteria in the body if antibiotics are taken.

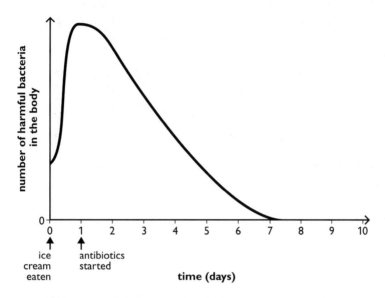

(a) (i) Explain why the sisters did not become unwell until the day after eating the ice cream. (1)

(ii) Tolani felt much better after taking the antibiotics for eight days. Explain why. (1)

(iii) Fumi is the older sister, and thinks she knows better! After four days she felt fine and so stopped taking the antibiotics. Two days later she was really ill again. Explain why this happened. (1)

(b) (i) Food poisoning can make a person vomit and have diarrhoea. This makes them lose water. Give **one** important function of water in the body. (1)

(ii) Vomiting can bring acid from the stomach into the mouth. How could this harm the teeth? (1)

(c) It is possible to give a vaccine against some types of bacteria that cause diarrhoea. How does a vaccine help to control infection by bacteria? (2)

6: Green plants as living organisms

6.1 Which option best completes each of the following sentences? (10)

(a) During photosynthesis a leaf uses

oxygen	carbon dioxide
starch	protein

(b) Root hair cells have a large surface area to

photosynthesise more efficiently	absorb minerals and water
make contact with other roots	store excess carbohydrate

(c) An animal cell does not have

a membrane	a nucleus
cytoplasm	chloroplasts

(d) A reagent that can be used to test for starch is

Universal Indicator	iodine solution
limewater	methylene blue

(e) A plant cell wall is made of

protein	starch
fat	cellulose

(f) The part of a flower that receives pollen from a visiting insect is the

stigma	petal
anther	sepal

(g) The roots of a small plant grow

towards light and against gravity	towards light and with gravity
with gravity and away from light	towards both light and water

(h) In the carbon cycle, bacteria and fungi are

producers	carnivores
decomposers	photosynthesisers

(i) An important mineral in the soil is

carbonate	sulphate
nitrogen	nitrate

(j) While it is dark, a plant

respires and photosynthesises

respires only, using oxygen

photosynthesises only, using carbon dioxide

respires only, using carbon dioxide

6.2 Amna used the apparatus shown below to measure how the concentration of carbon dioxide affected the rate of photosynthesis.

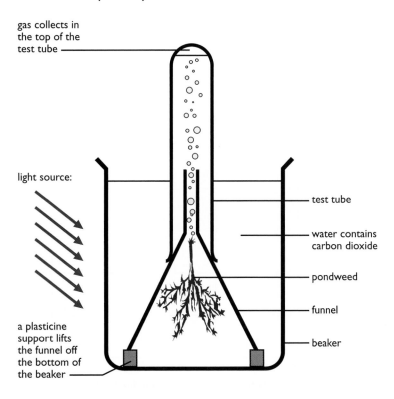

She obtained the following results:

concentration of carbon dioxide (%)	rate of photosynthesis (number of bubbles released per minute)
0.05	7
0.10	13
0.15	20
0.20	26
0.25	30
0.30	31
0.50	31

(a) (i) Plot the results from the table on the previous page on a grid like the one below. (4)

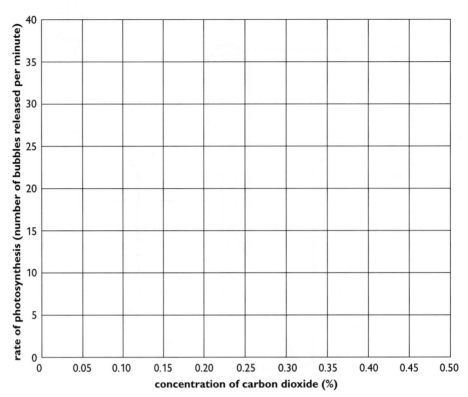

(ii) Use your graph to find at what concentration of carbon dioxide the plant produced 24 bubbles per minute? (1)

(iii) What does the graph tell you about how a greenhouse owner could grow his plants most efficiently? (2)

(b) When Amna carried out this investigation she wanted it to be a fair test. Name **three** factors which she should control for this to be true. (3)

(c) Amna thought that the gas given off by the plant was oxygen.

(i) How could she test if this was true? (1)

(ii) Amna's teacher said that the number of bubbles released was not an accurate way of measuring the rate of photosynthesis. How could Amna measure the volume of gas accurately? (1)

(iii) How could Amna make her results more reliable? (1)

6.3 Billy bought a potted plant for his grandma's birthday. She tried to look after it, but after a while she noticed that the leaves were turning yellow.

(a) (i) What is the name of the green pigment in plants? (1)

(ii) Which mineral is needed for the plant to make this pigment? (1)

(iii) What does the plant use the pigment for? (1)

(b) A potted plant is more likely to suffer from a mineral shortage than a plant growing in the garden. Explain why. (1)

(c) Billy wanted to buy some houseplant fertiliser for his grandma's plant. His science teacher said that he could mix his own, and suggested the following substances.

A NITRO-GROW $NH_4 NO_3$

B TUMMY-SALT $Mg SO_4$

C WHIZZBANG $K NO_3$

D SUPERPHOS $Ca(H_2PO_4)_2$

(i) Give the letter of one substance he would need to include to make sure that his fertiliser contained each of the following minerals (2)

potassium

phosphate

nitrate

magnesium

(ii) Sometimes excess nitrates in fertilisers can be washed into lakes and rivers. Give **two** reasons why this might be harmful to the lake or river. (2)

(iii) Some of the leaves fell off grandma's plant and lay on the soil beneath it. They slowly decomposed. Name **one** type of organism that might carry out this decomposition. (1)

6.4 This diagram shows a section through an insect-pollinated flower.

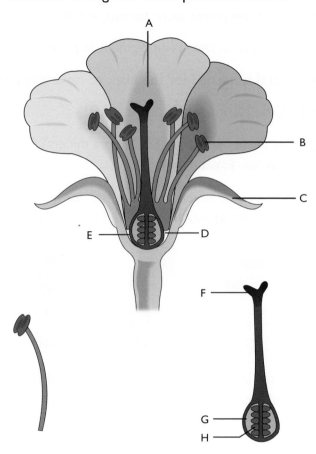

(a) Use the label letters to identify which part of the flower

   (i) makes the male sex cells (1)

   (ii) attracts insects (1)

   (iii) will eventually become a fruit (1)

   (iv) receives pollen (1)

(b) This paragraph is about the life cycle of plants. Copy and complete it by filling in the missing words, chosen from this list. (5)

dispersal	pollination
reproduction	fertilisation
germinates	grows

A young plant develops when a seed .... and matures until it produces a flower for .... Male gametes are transferred during the process of .... and join with female gametes during .... Eventually fruits are formed, and are separated from the parent plant during the process of ....

(c) Jack noticed that birds often eat seeds, and his teacher explained that the seeds contained food stores such as starch. Describe in detail how Jack could test that seeds contain starch. Include any **control** he would need to use, and give one **safety precaution** he should take. (4)

6.5 Hydrogencarbonate indicator solution changes colour according to changes in pH.

pH	colour of indicator
neutral or very slightly acidic	red
acidic	yellow
alkaline	purple

Five test tubes were set up as shown in the diagram below. Red hydrogencarbonate indicator solution was added to each of the tubes. The tubes were left on a sunny window ledge for three hours.

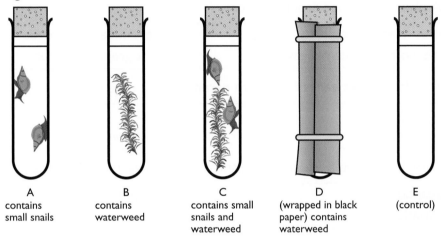

A
contains
small snails

B
contains
waterweed

C
contains small
snails and
waterweed

D
(wrapped in black
paper) contains
waterweed

E
(control)

(a) (i) Which acidic gas, produced by living organisms, is likely to affect the acidity of the indicator solution? (1)

(ii) After three hours what would be the colour of the indicator solution in test tube A? (1)

(iii) Explain your answer. (1)

(b) (i) What would be the colour of the indicator solution in tube B? (1)

(ii) Explain your answer. (1)

(iii) The colour of the indicator solution did not change in tube C. Explain why. (1)

(c) What was the purpose of the control (tube E)? (1)

7: Variation and classification

7.1 Which option best completes each of the following sentences? (10)

(a) Butterflies are insects because they

lay eggs	can fly
have three main body parts	feed on nectar

(b) The genes which control the characteristics of a cell are part of the

membrane	nucleus
cytoplasm	chloroplasts

(c) A plant is classified as a moss because it

lives near water	can produce many seeds
has no real roots or leaves	is dark green in colour

(d) A child receives genes from both parents at the time of

conception	ovulation
menstruation	fertilisation

(e) Polar bears have thick white fur, and live in snowy areas. This is an example of

adaptation	development
variation	growth

(f) Some animals move to new habitats when conditions are harsh. This is an example of

hibernation	variation
conservation	migration

(g) An eagle is a bird because it

has scales	has a beak
can fly	feeds on other birds

(h) Fungi are not included in the plant kingdom because they do not

reproduce	respire
photosynthesise	excrete

(i) Arranging living things into groups of related organisms is called

fertilisation	adaptation
variation	classification

(j) One of the following human characteristics is not affected by environment. It is

body mass	eye colour
height	arm strength

7.2   The drawings show mice from two different breeds.

(a) (i)   Give **two** ways in which the mice are different.   (2)

(ii)   These differences were inherited from their parents. What is the name of
the chemicals in the chromosomes that control these differences?   (1)

(iii) Which **two** types of cell pass this information from the parents to their
offspring?   (2)

| red blood cell | sperm cell | nerve cell |
| white blood cell | skin cell | egg cell |

(b) Freddy thought the colour differences between the mice were due to their diet. He
had one pair of mice that had a litter of sixteen babies, and decided to feed half of
them on a diet containing black pigment and the other half on a diet without the
pigment. He thought that he would be ready to collect his results after 28 days.

(i)   What is the **input** (independent) **variable** in this investigation?   (1)

(ii)   What is the **outcome** (dependent) **variable** in this investigation?   (1)

(iii) Suggest **two** other factors that Freddy should control to make sure that
this is a fair test.   (2)

(c) After 28 days Freddy observed that the two groups of mice showed no colour
differences. He concluded that the differences were due to which of the
following?   (1)

| genes and environment | environment only |
| genes only | chance only |

7.3   Living organisms can be classified according to characteristics they have.

(a) Which **three** of the following characteristics are likely to be the most useful
for classifying animals?   (3)

| the type of skin it has |
| how heavy it is |
| whether or not it has a bony skeleton |
| how fast it can run |
| how long it is |
| whether it has eyes or not |

(b) Copy the words in the boxes below and then draw lines to match the descriptions of living organisms with the name of the classification group. (5)

group	description of characteristics
spider	cells with a definite cell wall but no chlorophyll
insect	produces spores and cells contain chlorophyll
fungus	two body parts and eight jointed legs
fern	body is made of a single cell, with a clear nucleus and cytoplasm
protist	three body parts and six jointed legs

(c) (i) Give **one** way in which a bacterium differs from all of the above organisms. (1)

   (ii) Give **one** way in which a virus differs from a bacterium. (1)

7.4 Samir and Nisar were investigating certain features of other members of their year group at school.

(a) The first feature they investigated was whether each of their friends had 'joined' ear lobes or 'hanging' ear lobes.

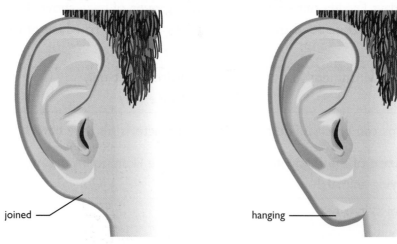

joined   hanging

They recorded their results in a table.

joined ear lobes	hanging ear lobes
22	8

Draw a chart like the one below and draw on a bar to show how many pupils had 'joined' ear lobes. (2)

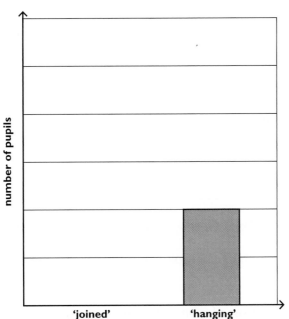

(b) Next they investigated the length of the forearm (from the elbow to the tip of the middle finger).

(i) Why was it important that each pupil kept their arm straight during the measurement? (1)

This bar chart shows their results.

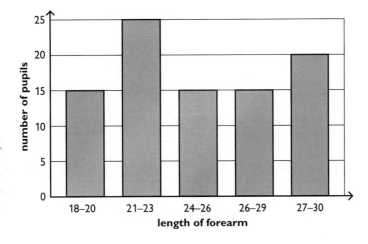

(ii) What units do you think they used for their measurements of forearm length? (1)

(iii) Give **one** mistake in the way they grouped the arm lengths in their bar chart. (1)

(c) Samir and Nisar also checked whether or not the pupils could roll their tongue into a U-shape. They found that the pupils either could do this or they could not. There was nobody who could 'half roll' their tongue, or 'three quarters roll' it. Copy the table below and then use a tick (✓) or a cross (✗) to complete the table. (2)

characteristic	inherited only	inherited and affected by the environment
shape of ear lobe		
length of forearm		
ability to roll tongue		

(d) Nisar said that the features they had investigated depended on the pupils' parents.

  (i) Explain how a child can look like both parents but **not** be identical to either of them. (2)

  (ii) There was one set of identical twins in the year group that they investigated. Why do identical twins have identical characteristics? (1)

7.5 A scientist working in Scotland believed that otters were so good at catching fish because they could keep their bodies warmer in cold water. He used very small data loggers to record the body temperatures of both fish and otters in water at different temperatures. This graph shows his results.

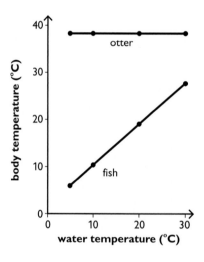

(a) Higher body temperatures speed up the action of enzymes involved in respiration and digestion, and make muscles more flexible. Explain why the scientist thought that the otters were at an advantage if the water was at only 5 °C. (3)

(b) The water temperature close to the outflow from a power station rose to 25 °C. What would happen to the body temperature of

    (i)   the otter? (1)

    (ii) the fish? (1)

(c) This diagram shows an otter.

    (i)   From the diagram give **two** ways in which the otter is adapted for swimming quickly underwater. (2)

    (ii) The otter is a mammal. Give **one** feature, not shown in the diagram, which is shared by all mammals. (1)

    (iii) The otter will eat frogs, grass snakes and even ducklings. Give **one** feature that is shared by otters, fish, frogs, snakes and ducklings. (1)

(d) The scientist noticed that not all of the fish were the same length, even though they looked the same otherwise. What is this an example of? (1)

8: Ecology and environment

8.1 Which option best completes each of the following sentences? (10)

(a) Fungi are

producers	decomposers
consumers	herbivores

(b) Plants increase the biomass in the environment through the process of

absorption	seed production
respiration	photosynthesis

(c) The flow of energy between living organisms is

an example of respiration	a pyramid of numbers
a food chain	photosynthesis

(d) A chemical used to control the population of an insect that feeds on crops is a

hormone	nutrient
fertiliser	pesticide

(e) A simple method of measuring a population uses a

ruler	quadrat
measuring cylinder	set square

(f) The final size of a population is not affected by

the original size of the population
competition for food
the number of disease-causing organisms
the number of predators

(g) The top carnivore in a habitat is always

a bird	very small
a fox	an animal

(h) Each of the following is an example of pollution except for

excess nitrates flowing into rivers
DDT being sprayed onto crops
woodland being cut down
sulphur dioxide being released from car engines

(i) The proportion of the Sun's energy used in photosynthesis is approximately

10%	30%	1%	80%

(j) A habitat does not provide

food	predators
breeding sites	shelter

8.2 The diagram shows part of a farmland food chain.

lettuce   snail   thrush   hawk

(a) The number of organisms at each stage of the food chain can be represented by a pyramid.

(i) Copy this pyramid and then write the name of each organism alongside the bars of the pyramid. (1)

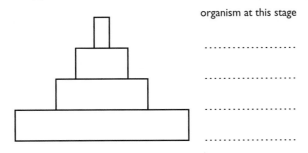

organism at this stage

....

....

....

....

(ii) The thrush has many ticks (small parasites) living under its feathers. Redraw the pyramid of numbers to show this. (2)

(b) The thrushes look for some of their food in gardens, and are often killed and eaten by cats. Explain the effect of this on **snails** and **lettuces**. (2)

(c) Farmers are encouraged to leave hedgerows around their fields. Suggest **two** reasons why this might increase the population of thrushes. (2)

8.3 The graph below shows how the population of wild trout in a lake changed over a period of time.

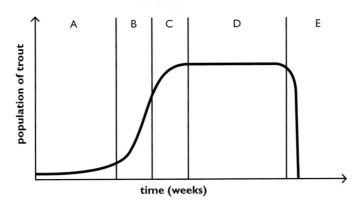

(a) (i) What does the section labelled D tell you about the birth rate and the death rate of the trout during this time period? (1)

(ii) Explain how you know this. (1)

(b) (i) Which part of the curve shows when the fish began to compete with each other for food? (1)

(ii) Explain how you know this. (1)

(iii) Suggest **one** other factor that might be affecting the population curve at this point. (1)

(c) A fish farmer decides to grow trout in enormous nets in a Scottish loch.
He provides the food for the trout, and then catches them for sale.

(i) He wants the trout to grow quickly. Which nutrient should the trout food contain to make sure that this happens? (1)

(ii) The trout food is expensive, and the fish farmer wants to make a profit.
A population of farmed trout will grow along the same curve as the population of wild trout shown in the graph. Which section of the population curve represents the best time for him to catch the fish for sale? (1)

(iii) Explain your answer. (2)

8.4 The diagram shows a food web in the sea close to Antarctica.

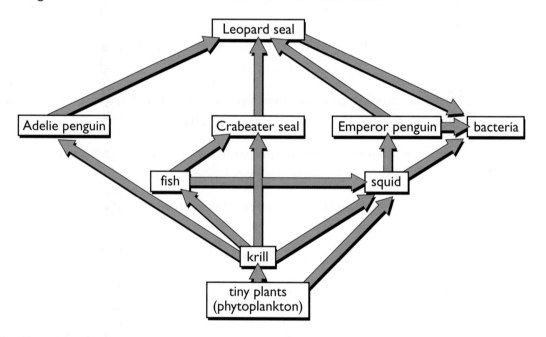

(a) (i) Identify an example of each of the following (4)

a herbivore

a producer

a carnivore

a decomposer

(ii) Draw out a food chain of five organisms selected from this food web. (2)

(b) Scientists are very concerned that oil drilling in Antarctica might release heavy metals such as mercury into the environment. They measured the levels of mercury in a number of members of this food web, and found that the Leopard Seal had very high values.

    (i) Explain how mercury builds up in an animal's tissues. (1)

    (ii) Explain why Leopard seals had the **highest** concentration of mercury in their tissues. (1)

(c) Emperor penguins feed on squid. Squid swim very quickly, and have a slippery skin.

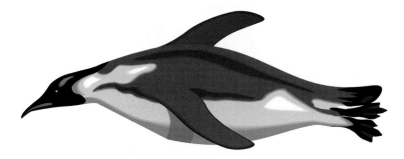

Suggest **two** ways in which the Emperor penguin is well adapted to catching its prey. (2)

8.5   Deforestation removes many tens of thousands of trees every year.

(a) Nearby farms are often flooded when forests have been cut in this way. Explain why. (1)

(b) Rainforests are important habitats for many animals. Give **two** reasons why fewer animals can survive if trees have been removed. (2)

45

(c) Fallen leaves and fruits from the cut trees can be decomposed.

    (i) Which type of organisms carry out this decomposition? (1)

    (ii) During decomposition heat is released. Which biological process is responsible for this release of energy during decomposition? (1)

    (iii) Some small forest lizards pile up the decomposing leaves over their eggs. This incubates the eggs until the young lizards hatch out. The proportion of male and female lizards that hatch is affected by the temperature of incubation. Biologists have collected eggs and incubated them at different temperatures. The results are shown in the table below.

temperature (°C)	percentage of lizards hatching as males	percentage of lizards hatching as females
26	0	100
28	0	100
30	0	100
32	21	79
34	78	22
36	100	0
38	100	0

Plot these results on a grid like the one below. (3)

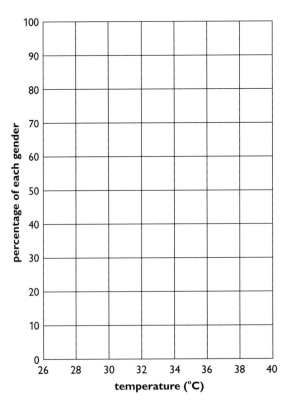

46

(iv) Conservationists want to release the lizards back into a suitable habitat. They would like to release one male for every female. Why do they need to release males and females in equal numbers? (1)

(v) Use the graph to estimate the temperature at which 50% of the hatching lizards will be male and 50% will be female. (1)

8.6 Copy the words in the boxes below and then draw lines to match up each term with the best description. There are more descriptions than terms! (4)

ecological term

description

| all the members of the same species living in one area |

| nitrate |

| managing the environment for the benefit of wildlife |

| competition |

| needed by plants in the habitat to make chlorophyll |

| population |

| a mineral often added to farmland in fertilisers |

| conservation |

| two or more organisms are trying to obtain the same thing from their environment |

Chemistry

9: Experiments in chemistry

9.1   Which option best completes each of the following sentences?   (10)

(a)   A colourless gas which turns limewater milky is

oxygen	carbon monoxide
hydrogen	carbon dioxide

(b)   The presence of water can be detected using cobalt chloride paper. If water is present, cobalt chloride paper turns

from blue to white	from pink to blue
from white to blue	from blue to pink

(c)   A dangerous gas which smells like rotten eggs is

chlorine	hydrogen sulphide
carbon monoxide	ammonia

(d)   Anhydrous copper sulphate can be used to test for water. If water is present, anhydrous copper sulphate turns from

blue to white	blue to black
blue to pink	white to blue

(e)   A colourless gas which will relight a glowing splint is

oxygen	carbon monoxide
hydrogen	carbon dioxide

(f)   2350 cm^3 is the same volume as

235 ml	23.5 litres
2.35 dm^3	0.235 litres

(g)   The hottest part of a Bunsen flame is

bright yellow	pale blue
deep blue	red-orange

(h)   A factor that a student chooses to change during the course of an experiment is

a fixed variable	an independent variable
a controlled variable	a dependent variable

(i)   A gas that is released when zinc reacts with hydrochloric acid burns with a 'pop'. The gas is

chlorine	oxygen
hydrogen	carbon dioxide

(j)   A piece of apparatus used to measure and transfer small volumes of liquids is a

burette	pipette
measuring cylinder	evaporating dish

9.2 Jane was interested in how people measured time in the past. She made two candles, and drew lines on them.

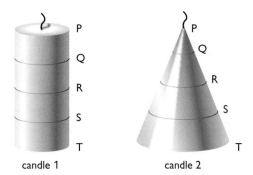

candle 1   candle 2

(a) (i) What would Jane use to measure the volume of wax she used in making the candles? (1)

(ii) What would Jane use to measure the distance between the lines? (1)

(b) Jane's idea was to time how long it took for the candles to burn. She burned candle 1 first, and presented her results in this table.

section that was burned	time taken to burn (minutes)
P to Q	20
Q to R	20
R to S	
S to T	20

(i) Jane drew a graph of her results. The points are plotted on the graph grid below.

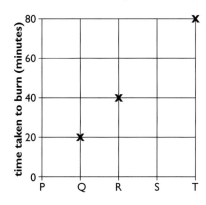

Draw a graph like the one above, and then add the missing value on the graph and join the points. (1)

49

(ii) Jane then burned candle 2.

Draw another line on your graph, showing roughly how long you think it took for candle 2 to burn between the sections. (1)

(c) Jane thought that the candles could be used to measure time throughout the country. Suggest **three** features of the candles which would have to be kept constant if the candles were going to be reliable timekeepers. (3)

9.3 Neel used this apparatus to find out which substances are released when ethanol is burned.

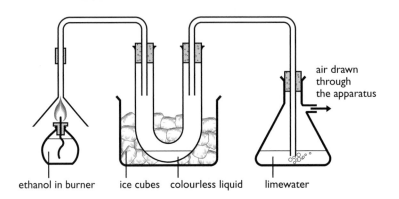

ethanol in burner   ice cubes   colourless liquid   limewater

(a) (i) Why did he add ice cubes around the U-tube? (1)

(ii) One of the gases turned the limewater milky. What is the name of this gas? (1)

(iii) What test should Neel carry out on the colourless liquid in the U-tube? What do you think a positive result would be, and what would the result tell him? (2)

(b) Ethylene glycol is another alcohol, and it is sometimes used in antifreeze. It can be added to the contents of a car radiator to prevent the water freezing as the temperature falls.

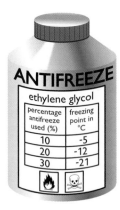

(i) There are two hazard warning symbols on the label of the antifreeze container. What **two** precautions would you take if you were using this antifreeze? (2)

(ii) The label on the container also provides information about the effect of the antifreeze on the freezing point of water. Neel had filled his radiator with 2 litres of solution containing 200 cm³ of antifreeze and 1800 cm³ of water. During the night the temperature fell to 255 K. What would happen to Neel's radiator? Explain your answer. (3)

9.4 (a) Match the following hazard symbols with their descriptions. (Write A = , B = etc.) There are more descriptions than symbols. (5)

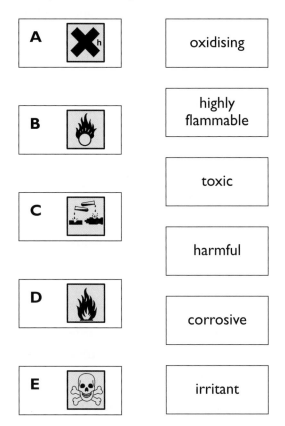

(b) Chemicals may have more than one hazard warning. Which hazards are identified on this petrol container? (3)

9.5 Jenna and Saed were investigating the heating power of Bunsen burners. They began by checking whether the burner delivered more heat with the air hole open or with it closed. They measured the heat energy from the Bunsen burner by finding out the time taken for some water to boil.

(a) (i) What is the **input** (independent) **variable** in this experiment? (1)

(ii) What is the **outcome** (dependent) **variable** in this experiment? (1)

(b) Which of the following variables should be controlled to make this a fair test? Which of the following are the **three** most important choices. (3)

the position of the Bunsen burner below the beaker
the thermometer which was used
the volume of water in the beaker
the science lab in which they were working
the time of day
the position of the gas tap (i.e. how much flow of gas)

9.6 This question involves identification of gases. Use the information provided to copy and complete the table below. Choose from the following gases: (5)

oxygen   hydrogen   ammonia
carbon dioxide   sulphur dioxide

effect on limewater	pH with Universal Indicator	effect on a burning splint	gas
none	4	puts it out	
none	7	goes 'pop'	
turns it cloudy	6	puts it out	
none	7	burns more brightly	
none	8	puts it out	

52

9.7   Look at these diagrams.

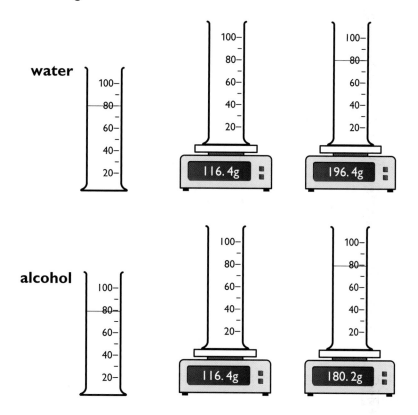

(a) (i)   Calculate the density of water and of alcohol. Show your working.   (3)

     (ii) If a mixture of alcohol and water is allowed to stand for a long time, the
           alcohol will float to the top. Name a piece of apparatus that will allow you
           to remove a small volume of alcohol.   (1)

(b) Draw diagrams of the arrangement of apparatus you would use to investigate
     whether temperature affects the production of crystals of copper sulphate from
     a copper sulphate solution.   (4)

10: Solids, liquids and gases

10.1 Which option best completes each of the following sentences? (10)

(a) When a solid melts, the particles

vibrate more	vibrate to the same extent
vibrate less	stop vibrating completely

(b) Salty water

freezes at 0 °C	doesn't freeze
freezes above 0 °C	freezes below 0 °C

(c) The change of water from liquid to water vapour is

boiling	evaporation
freezing	condensation

(d) During the water cycle, the change of water vapour to droplets of liquid water is

evaporation	precipitation
condensation	boiling

(e) In an experiment to investigate the effect of temperature on evaporation, temperature is

a fixed variable	the outcome variable
the control	the input variable

(f) Particles move through liquids and gases by

concentration	dilution
diffusion	dispersal

(g) Density can be defined as

mass × volume	$\dfrac{mass}{volume}$
$\dfrac{volume}{mass}$	$\dfrac{mass^2}{volume}$

(h) Adding impurities to water causes its boiling point to

lower	stay the same
rise	rise to twice its original level

(i) The temperature at which a liquid changes to a gas is the

freezing point	boiling point
condensation point	sublimation point

(j) During a change of state, the mass of a substance

remains the same
rises
falls
may or may not change depending on the two states involved

10.2 Some solid wax was slowly warmed in a boiling tube. The temperature of the wax during the warming process was measured using a temperature sensor connected to a data logger.

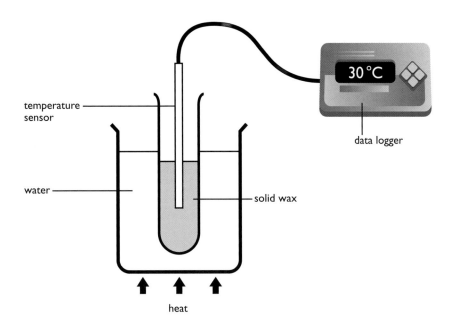

A graph of the results looked like this:

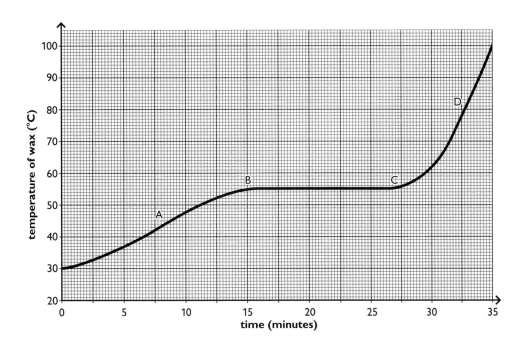

(a) (i) At what point on the graph (A, B, C or D) did the wax begin to change state? (1)

(ii) Explain your answer. (2)

(iii) What is the physical state of the wax at point D? (1)

(b) Suggest **two** advantages of carrying out the investigation using a temperature sensor and data logger rather than a thermometer. (2)

(c) This particular wax boils at 275 °C. Why can the wax not boil during this investigation? (1)

(d) Describe and explain the differences between the movement of the water molecules at the start and the end of the investigation. (2)

10.3 The diagram below shows a can of pressurised propane, used as a fuel for burning paint from wooden window frames. Most of the propane in the can is in the liquid state, but some of it is gas.

PROPO
GAS

(a) (i) What happens to the pressure inside the can when the temperature falls? Explain your answer. (2)

(ii) What would happen to the flame from the paint burner if the painter were using it out of doors on a cold day? (1)

(iii) There is a warning on the can not to throw it into a fire. Why is this important? (1)

(b) Which of these statements about the propane liquid in the can are correct? (3)

The molecules of the liquid are

smaller than	
the same distance apart as	
closer together than	
moving faster than	than those in the gas
the same size as	
bigger than	
further apart than	
moving more slowly	

10.4 Many motorway bridges are made from concrete. The concrete is positioned in sections, with small gaps between them.

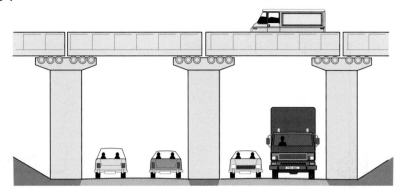

(a) (i)   What happens to the size of most objects when the temperature rises?   (1)

   (ii)   As the temperature rises, what will happen to the gaps between the concrete sections?   (1)

   (iii) If there were no gaps between the concrete sections, what might happen if the temperature rises?   (1)

(b) The gaps between the concrete sections are filled with tar which becomes soft when it gets warm. Why is it important that the tar becomes soft?   (1)

(c) When it rains the gaps may become filled with water. Explain why this might be dangerous if the temperature falls below 0 °C.   (1)

10.5 Sulphur is an element which can exist as a solid, a liquid or a gas. The diagram below shows sulphur in different states, and the letters A, B, C and D represent changes of state between solid, liquid and gas.

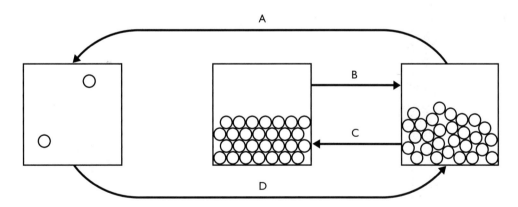

(i)   What is change of state A called?   (1)

(ii) What is change of state B called?   (1)

(iii) What is change of state C called?   (1)

(iv) What is change of state D called?   (1)

10.6 The volume of an object can be found by the displacement of water, and its mass can be found using a weighing machine. Juno wanted to find out if her brooch was made of silver, and so made the following measurements.

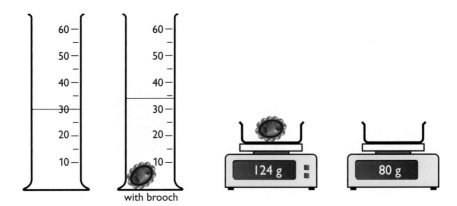

with brooch

(i) Calculate the volume of the brooch. Show your working. (2)

(ii) Calculate the mass of the brooch. Show your working. (1)

(iii) Calculate the density of the brooch. Show your working. (2)

(iv) Silver has a density of 10.2 g/cm³, lead has a density of 11.5 g/cm³, and nickel has a density of 8.9 g/cm³. Is the brooch silver? (1)

10.7 Racing motorcycle tyres must run at the correct pressure, or grip will be lost. The tyres are inflated with air, and then kept warm before the race begins.

(i) What causes the air pressure inside the tyre? (1)

(ii) Why does the pressure increase when the pit crew pump up the tyre? (1)

(iii) What happens to the air pressure inside the tyre when the tyre warmers are put on before the race? Explain your answer. (1)

(iv) The ride on the motorcycle is much more comfortable if the tyres are inflated with air than if solid tyres are used. Explain why this is the case. (1)

10.8 All the pupils in the class decided to celebrate their teacher's retirement. They bought a lot of rubber party balloons, and wrapped the balloons in coloured aluminium foil. They filled half with helium and the other half with air. Each balloon contained exactly the same volume of gas.

(a) Explain why the air-filled balloons drop to the ground but the helium-filled balloons rise. (2)

(b) The diagram below shows a number of arrangements of particles.

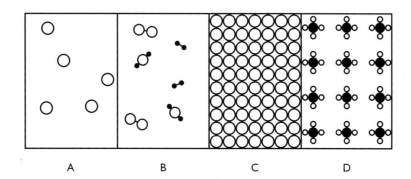

Which letter represents

(i) the helium gas (1)

(ii) the aluminium foil (1)

(c) Over a period of a week the balloons shrink because the particles of gas escape. The helium-filled balloons shrink more quickly.

(i) Name the process by which the particles of gas move. (1)

(ii) Why does helium escape more quickly than air from a balloon? (1)

11: Mixtures, separation and solubility

11.1 Which option best completes each of the following sentences? (5)

(a) Pure water is

a solution	a compound
a mixture	an element

(b) A mixture made of a solvent and an insoluble substance is

a solution	a suspension
an oil	a solute

(c) The change of state from liquid to gas is

condensation	melting
distillation	evaporation

(d) A separation method that separates a solid from a liquid by careful pouring is

distillation	filtration
decanting	evaporation

(e) An example of a mixture is

iron filings	air
water	sodium chloride

11.2 Jack had a leaking ballpoint pen, which left a stain on his trouser pocket.

His science teacher rubbed some ethanol on to the stain with a tissue, and noticed that the tissue developed a purple stain and the stain on his trousers became lighter.

(a) Explain how the ethanol helped to remove the stain. (2)

(b) The teacher asked Jack whether he thought that the ballpoint ink was made of one type of dye or several.

　　(i) Name the technique that Jack could use to find out. (1)

(ii) Jack obtained the following results:

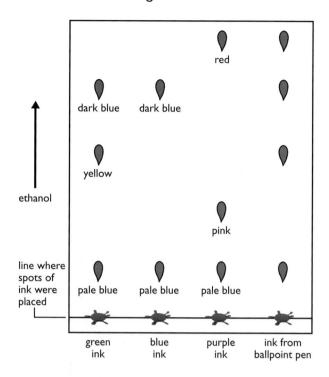

Which colours were present in the ballpoint ink? (1)

(iii) How many coloured substances were there in the blue ink?
How do you know? (1)

(iv) Which word is the best one to describe each coloured substance? (1)

solution	solvent
solute	suspension

11.3 Saara and David were investigating the effect of solute concentration on the boiling point of water. They measured out different masses of salt and dissolved each sample in a different 500 cm³ of water. They then measured and recorded the temperature at which the water boiled.

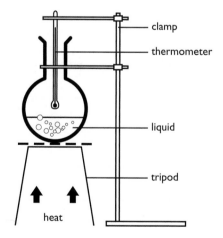

(a) (i) What is the **independent** (input) **variable** in their investigation? (1)

(ii) What is the **dependent** (outcome) **variable** in their investigation? (1)

(iii) They had a list of possible **fixed** (controlled) **variables**. From this list choose **two** which must be controlled, and **one** which would have little or no effect on their results. (3)

volume of water	type of salt dissolved in water
starting temperature of water	room temperature

(b) They wrote down their results in this table.

mass of salt added (g)	boiling point (°C)
0	100
10	100.6
20	103
30	104
40	106
50	result lost
60	109.2

(i) Plot their results on a grid like the one below. (3)

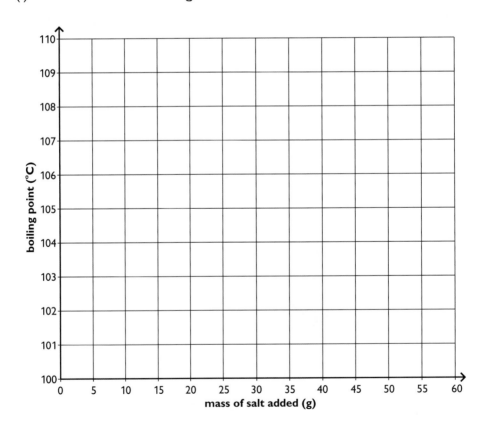

(ii) From your graph, suggest a likely result for the one, at 50 g of salt added, which they lost. (1)

(iii) Predict the temperature at which a solution of 100 g of salt in 500 cm³ of water would boil. Show your working. (2)

11.4 Sally added some potassium manganate crystals to a beaker of water.

heat

(a) (i) How could she see that some of the crystals had dissolved in the water? (1)

(ii) What could she do to increase the amount of the potassium manganate which dissolved? (1)

(b) How could Sally collect potassium manganate crystals from the solution in the beaker? (1)

(c) Sally carried out an experiment to investigate how much of three food flavourings will dissolve in water at different temperatures. The results are shown in the graph below.

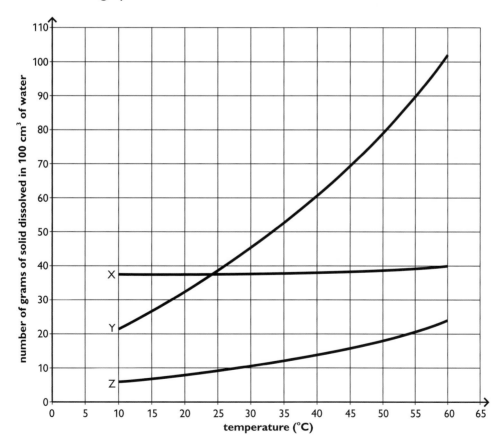

(i) How many grams of flavouring Z dissolved in the water at 40 °C? (1)

(ii) Which flavouring dissolved best at 20 °C? (1)

(iii) Which **two** flavourings are equally soluble at 24 °C? (1)

11.5 Match each of these terms with its correct definition. Draw a straight line between the term and the definition. (3)

term	definition
concentrated	a mixture of a solvent and a solute
saturated	the liquid part of a solution
solution	a solution with many solute particles in a small volume of solvent
solvent	the amount of a substance that will dissolve in a liquid
solubility	able to dissolve
soluble	a solution that cannot accept any more solute

11.6 Abi added some sugar to 100 cm³ of cold water in a beaker. She stirred the water to dissolve the sugar, and then added more sugar until no more would dissolve.

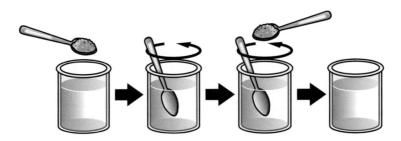

She repeated the experiment with salt, curry powder and instant coffee. Each time, she used a different beaker containing 100 cm³ of cold water. The results are shown in the bar chart below.

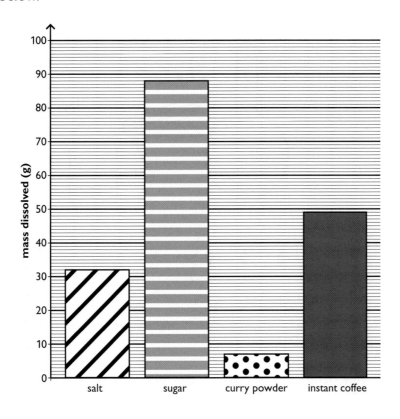

(a) (i) State **two** ways in which Abi made this a fair test. (2)

   (ii) Which substance was the least soluble in water? (1)

   (iii) How many times more soluble was sugar than salt? Give your answer to 1 decimal place, and show your working. (3)

(b) When Abi makes a cup of coffee for her father, the coffee dissolves much more quickly. Explain why. (1)

11.7 A science teacher set up the apparatus shown below, with a solution of a water-soluble food dye in the flask.

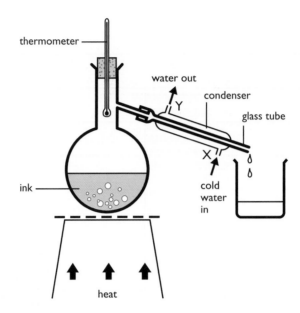

(a) (i) What is the name of the separation process which the teacher is demonstrating? (1)

(ii) During the demonstration, which pair of processes will occur? (1)

melting then evaporation	condensation then evaporation
melting then boiling	evaporation then condensation

(b) The teacher says that the liquid which is collected in the beaker is pure water. Describe **one** test which would show the liquid is **water**, and another test which would show that it is **pure water**. (2)

(c) (i) Water at 20 °C enters the condenser at X. Predict the temperature of the water when it leaves the condenser at Y. (1)

(ii) Explain your answer. (1)

(iii) Give **two** ways in which the water vapour is changed as it passes down the glass tube in the condenser. (2)

11.8 The following are different ways of separating the components of mixtures.

A fractional distillation   B simple distillation
C with a magnet   D chromatography
E filtration

Choose one of the letters to show which is the best method to obtain

(a) iron from a mixture of iron filings and sulphur

(b) water from seawater

(c) alcohol from wine

(d) food colourings from sweets (4)

12: Acids, bases and indicators

12.1 Which option best completes each of the following? (10)

(a) A substance that can attack other materials, including human skin, is

basic	strong
corrosive	an indicator

(b) A substance that gives up hydrogen in a chemical reaction is

a base	a metal
an acid	an alkali

(c) A chemical reaction between an alkali or base and an acid is

a neutralisation	an indication
an oxidation	a decomposition

(d) A solution with a pH of 7 is

acidic	corrosive
basic	neutral

(e) One product of a neutralisation reaction is

an acid	a salt
an alkali	an indicator

(f) A compound that reacts with an acid to release carbon dioxide is

a base	carbon monoxide
a carbonate	a metal chloride

(g) A gas that turns limewater milky is

hydrogen	oxygen
nitrogen	carbon dioxide

(h) Acids react with metals to produce

salt + water	water vapour
salt + hydrogen	salt + carbon dioxide

(i) An alkali will always turn

litmus paper red	litmus paper blue
Universal Indicator yellow	limewater milky

(j) The sour taste of yoghurt is due to

tannic acid	lactic acid
hydrochloric acid	citric acid

12.2 Hydrochloric acid is an example of a strong acid, and is produced in the stomach during the digestion of food.

(a) A student added five drops of hydrochloric acid to a small volume of Universal Indicator solution in a test tube.

(i) What colour is the mixture of indicator and hydrochloric acid likely to be? (1)

(ii) Suggest a likely value for the pH of the hydrochloric acid. (1)

(b) Too much hydrochloric acid produced in the stomach can be a cause of indigestion. Magcarb indigestion tablets contain magnesium carbonate, and can be crushed into a powder. If the powder is added to hydrochloric acid in a test tube the mixture will fizz.

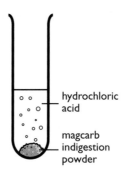

hydrochloric acid

magcarb indigestion powder

(i) Copy and complete the word equation for the reaction which is occurring. (2)

hydrochloric acid + ... → . . . . + ... + water

(ii) Use this equation to explain why the mixture fizzed after addition of the powdered tablets. (1)

(iii) The student continued to add powder to the acid, and noticed that the mixture stopped fizzing. Why did the fizzing stop? (1)

(c) Which of the following words could be used to describe magnesium carbonate? (2)

a solvent	a salt	a mixture
an element	an indicator	a compound

12.3 Scientists believe that acid rain is caused by gases in the atmosphere. An investigation into the formation of acid rain was carried out by collecting a number of gases. Each of the gases was bubbled through a sample of green, neutral Universal Indicator solution.

(a) Three of the gases caused the indicator to change colour. Once all the gas samples had been bubbled through the indicator, alkali was added, from a syringe, until the Universal Indicator changed back to green.

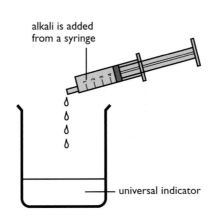

alkali is added
from a syringe

universal indicator

The results are shown in the table below.

gas collected	change in colour of indicator	volume of alkali needed to return indicator to green colour (cm³)
air	no change	0
carbon dioxide from burning coal	green to red	6.9
exhaust gases from an idling car	green to red	1.2
methane from a refuse tip	no change	0
human breath	green to yellow	0.2

(i)   Which gases formed neutral solutions?   (2)

Explain your answer.   (1)

(ii) Which gas produced the most acidic solution?   (1)

Explain your answer.   (1)

(iii) What is the name given to a reaction between an acid and an alkali?   (1)

(b) (i) Some metals used in buildings may react with acids in the air.
Copy and complete this word equation for this reaction.   (2)

copper + hydrochloric acid → .... + ...

(ii) Bronze statues often change to a green colour after many years of
exposure to the air. Use this word equation to explain why.   (2)

12.4 Wasps and bees are both insects which defend themselves using stings. The 'sting' involves the injection of a solution through the skin. The pH values of the 'stings' are shown below.

bee sting pH 2

wasp sting pH 10

(a) Copy and complete the table below to show whether the stings are acid or alkaline, and suggest what colour they would change Universal Indicator solution to. (4)

	acid or alkaline	colour of indicator solution
wasp sting		
bee sting		

(b) Some common household substances can be used to neutralise wasp and bee stings. Six of these substances are shown in the table below.

substance	pH value
water	7
washing soda	11
baking soda	8
bicarbonate toothpaste	8
vinegar	5
lemon juice	3

Give the name of one substance in the table which could neutralise

(i) a wasp sting (1)

(ii) a bee sting (1)

(c) Why is it useful that toothpaste is slightly alkaline? (2)

(d) Nettle leaves contain small cells which release formic acid.

(i) Suggest why dock leaves can be used to get rid of the irritation from a nettle sting. (1)

(ii) Why do you think that the relief from the sting is quicker if the dock leaf is crushed up before it is used in this way? (1)

12.5 Jack placed a conical flask on a pan balance. The flask weighed 100 g. He added 50 g of dilute hydrochloric acid and 5.0 g of calcium carbonate to the flask. The total mass of the flask and its contents was 155 g.

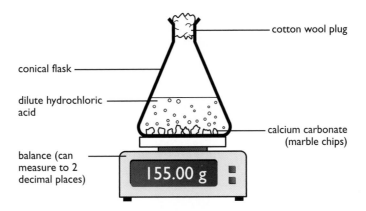

(a) The calcium carbonate and the hydrochloric acid quickly reacted together.
Copy and complete the word equation for the reaction which took place. (3)

calcium carbonate + hydrochloric acid → . . . . + ... + ...

(b) When the reaction stopped, the total mass had decreased from 155.00 g to 152.70 g. Some water had evaporated from the beaker. What other reason is there for the mass to fall in this way? (1)

(c) How did Jack know that the reaction had stopped? (1)

(d) At the end of the reaction, the calcium carbonate had neutralised the acid. Jack tested a few drops from the flask with Universal Indicator paper. What is the colour of the Universal Indicator paper after this test? (1)

(e) Calcium carbonate is a very common compound. Which of the materials in this list are mainly calcium carbonate? (3)

marble	limestone	sand
glass	chalk	
coal	glass	

(f) Metals also react with acids.

(i) Which gas is produced when a metal reacts with an acid? (1)

(ii) How would you test for this gas? (1)

12.6 The pH of a soil sample can be tested by shaking the soil with water, letting the particles settle and then adding Universal Indicator solution.

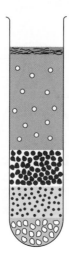

This table shows the pH values of six soil samples.

sample	pH value
A	8.0
B	7.5
C	7.0
D	8.0
E	4.5
F	6.0

(a) Which soil sample would give a green colour with the Universal Indicator solution? (1)

(b) Cauliflower and sprouts grow better in alkaline soil. In which soil samples should cauliflower and sprouts grow well? (1)

(c) Rhododendron is a shrub which grows better in acidic soils. In which of the soil samples would the rhododendron grow well? (1)

(d) Crushed limestone can be dissolved in water to produce calcium hydroxide. This calcium hydroxide (slaked lime) is sometimes added to acidic soils. Name the type of reaction which takes place between the lime and the soil. (1)

12.7 Sodium hydrogencarbonate (often called bicarbonate of soda) is present in baking powder.

(a) Which of these properties of sodium hydrogencarbonate are especially important for its use as baking powder? (2)

it is very soluble in water
it is not poisonous
it is a white solid
it does not have a smell
it forms a weak alkaline solution

(b) Baking powder also contains citric acid. When the baking powder is added to water, the acid and the hydrogencarbonate react together. Explain how this helps to give a light texture to cakes. (1)

13: Elements and compounds

13.1 Which option best completes each of the following sentences?   (5)

(a) A typical metal

is not a good conductor of electricity	
does not have a high melting point	
is not usually dull in appearance	
is not malleable	

(b) A substance made of only one type of atom is

pure	likely to be of low density
an element	an alloy

(c) The particles in a liquid are likely to be

in a regular fixed pattern	moving slightly
not moving	far apart

(d) Copper reacts with oxygen to produce

a gas	an acid
an oxide	an element

(e) When three or more different elements combine, and the third one is oxygen, the name of the compound will always end in

-ide	-ate
-gen	-ite

13.2 This table gives the number of protons, electrons and neutrons in some atoms and ions. The letters in the table are NOT the chemical symbols of the elements.

atom or ion	protons	neutrons	electrons
A	9	10	10
B	17	18	17
C	8	8	8
D	20	22	18
E	17	19	17
F	10	10	10

(a) Give the letter of   (5)

(i) a positive ion

(ii) a negative ion

(iii) a very reactive metal

(iv) a non-metal

(v) an atom or ion with an atomic number of 20

13.3 A group of pupils carried out a class practical in which they burned magnesium in air. They wished to record the mass of magnesium used and any change in the mass as burning took place.

(a) Draw and label a set of apparatus they might use to carry out this investigation. (3)

(b) The results are shown in the table below.

pupil	mass of magnesium (g)	mass of product (g)
Jack	6.4	10.4
Sam	3.8	6.5
Neela	4.8	8.4
Anja	6.1	10.7
James	2.7	4.0
Billy	4.2	7.0

(i) What is the name of the product which is formed? (1)

(ii) Present the results from the table above on a grid like the one below. Draw a line of best fit. (4)

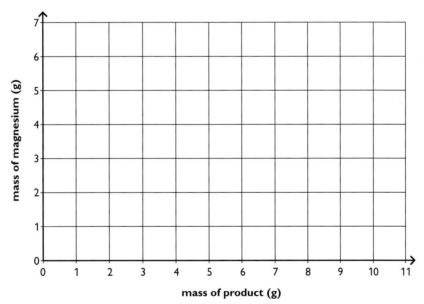

(iii) Use the graph to predict the mass of magnesium required to provide 7.5 g of product. (1)

(iv) Use the graph to predict how much product will be formed if 5.5 g of magnesium is burned in air. (1)

(v) Give one conclusion you can draw about the relationship between the mass of magnesium burned and the mass of product formed. (2)

13.4 The drawings show different elements that have been used to produce different objects.

(a) Copy the words in the boxes below and then draw lines to match the element to the reason for using it. (5)

element used   **reason for choosing this element**

aluminium in saucepans

it is lighter than air

silver for a necklace

it is a good conductor of heat

mercury in a barometer

it conducts electricity and is easy to stretch

helium in a balloon

it stays shiny because it does not react with oxygen in air

copper in cables

it stays liquid at room temperature

(b) Elements may have more than one use.

(i) Name **two** properties of copper that would make it suitable for use in the solid base of expensive saucepans. (2)

(ii) Name a property of helium that makes it suitable for storage in metal cylinders. (1)

13.5 The diagram shows a simplified Periodic Table. (The letters are NOT the symbols of the elements.)

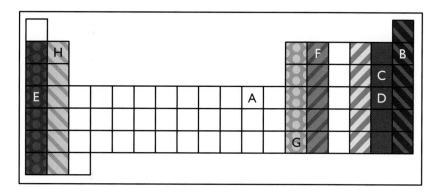

(a) Which letter is likely to be a metallic element? (1)

(b) Which letter is likely to be a very unreactive gas? (1)

(c) Magnesium chloride is formed when magnesium and chlorine combine together in a chemical reaction. Write the symbols for magnesium and chlorine. (2)

(d) The formula for a substance is FeS. What is the name of this substance? (1)

(e) Calcium burns brightly in oxygen, forming calcium oxide (CaO). Calcium oxide reacts with water, forming a compound with the formula $Ca(OH)_2$.

(i) Name the compound with the formula $Ca(OH)_2$. (1)

(ii) This compound is slightly soluble in water. Predict the colour of Universal Indicator when mixed with the solution. (1)

(iii) Why is $Ca(OH)_2$ not found in the Periodic Table? (1)

13.6 John Dalton used symbols like the ones shown here to represent atoms.

Some possible combinations of these atoms are shown in these diagrams.

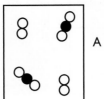 A

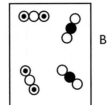 B

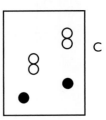 C

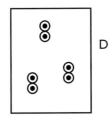 D

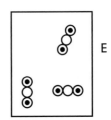 E

(a) (i) Give the letter which shows a mixture of an element and a compound. (1)

(ii) Give the letter which shows only a compound. (1)

(b) Give **one** difference between a compound and a mixture. (1)

(c) (i) Suggest a name and formula for the substance represented in D. (1)

(ii) Suggest names and formulae for the substances represented in C. (2)

13.7 Scientists were collecting material from the bottom of the Pacific Ocean. One of them believed that he had found a new metallic element – he called it Oceanium.

(a) Which **two** properties suggest that Oceanium could be a metal? (2)

it glows in the dark
it is a green solid
it has a high melting point
it is a good conductor of heat and electricity
it does not stick to a magnet

(b) One of the scientists washed the solid very carefully with pure water. The result was a blue solution with green solids floating in it.

(i) Name **one** method he could use to now separate the solid (Oceanium) from the solution. (1)

(ii) Name **one** method he could use to collect crystals from the solution. (1)

(iii) The green solid was found to react with a yellow gas. Suggest what this gas is, and suggest a name for the compound formed. (2)

14: Chemical reactions

14.1 Which option best completes each of the following sentences? (10)

(a) Each of the following is a sign that a chemical reaction has taken place except for

heat being released	the reaction being reversible
a new substance being formed	fizzing often occurring as a gas is formed

(b) The products of fermentation do not include

carbon dioxide	heat	glucose	ethanol

(c) A substance which will not decompose on heating is

copper sulphate	copper
copper oxide	copper carbonate

(d) If a hydrocarbon is burned in air, the products are

carbon dioxide + water	carbon dioxide + carbon monoxide
carbon + water	carbon monoxide + water

(e) When potassium manganate (VII) is heated, the following reaction occurs:

potassium manganate (VII) → potassium manganate (III)
+ oxygen + manganese dioxide

This is an example of

oxidation	decomposition
sublimation	combustion

(f) A chemical reaction between a metal and the air that takes place without burning is

decomposition	reduction
combustion	corrosion

(g) The reaction between iron and sulphur is exothermic, which means that it

consumes heat energy	releases heat
releases light	involves change in colour

(h) Hydrochloric acid and magnesium oxide react together to produce magnesium chloride and water. This type of reaction is an example of

reduction	oxidation
neutralisation	recombination

(i) Each of the following is a fossil fuel except for

natural gas	oil	coal	wood

(j) Spoilage of food is an example of a harmful chemical reaction. Food cannot be preserved by

adding extra water	removing oxygen
drying	keeping food in acidic conditions

14.2 Plants need nitrogen to grow well. Farmers add nitrogen-containing fertilisers to soil to increase crop yield. The fertilisers are manufactured chemically.

(a) (i)   Complete this equation for the production of fertiliser.   (2)

. . . . + ammonium hydroxide → ammonium nitrate +. . . . .

(ii)   What type of chemical reaction is this?   (1)

(b) Scientists in an agricultural laboratory investigated how the mass of ammonium hydroxide decreased during this reaction. They presented their results in the form of a graph.

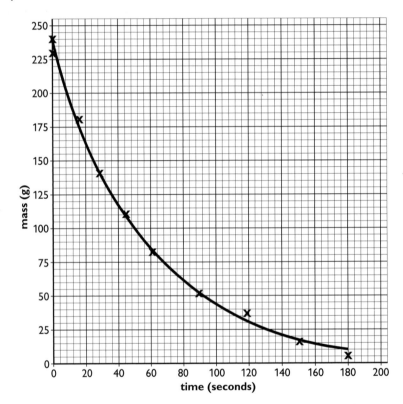

(i)   Over which 30 s period did the mass of ammonium hydroxide decrease most quickly?   (1)

(ii)   The mass of ammonium hydroxide was 240 g at the start. How long did it take for the mass to decrease by 75%? Show your working.   (2)

14.3 A science teacher heated iron filings and sulphur on a tray.

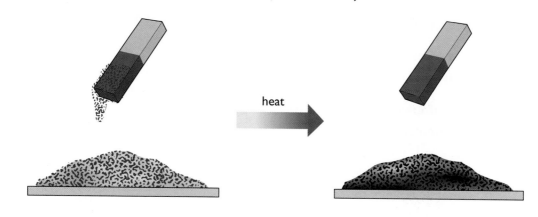

(a) (i) Write out an equation for this reaction. (1)

(ii) From the information in the diagram give **one** piece of evidence that a chemical reaction has occurred. (1)

(b) (i) Suggest the name and the formula for the solid formed when **zinc** is heated with sulphur. (2)

(ii) Some fossil fuels contain sulphur. When fossil fuels burn, sulphur reacts with oxygen. Write out a word equation for this reaction. (1)

(iii) What **type** of chemical reaction is this? (1)

14.4 This apparatus can be used to burn magnesium ribbon in air. The process was demonstrated by a science teacher.

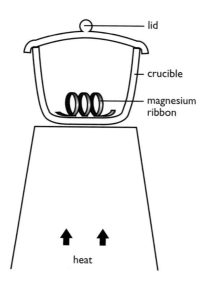

(a) (i) Explain why the teacher told the pupils that they should never look directly at burning magnesium. (1)

(ii) The teacher wanted to make a note of the changes in mass during the reaction. He told the pupils that he was going to gently rub the magnesium ribbon with a piece of abrasive paper before beginning the experiment. Why was this important? (1)

(b) The following results were obtained:

mass of crucible (g)	50	50	50	
mass of crucible + magnesium ribbon (g)	63	61	62	
mass of crucible + contents after heating (g)	69.8	70.1	70.1	

(i) Copy and complete the table by writing in the mean values for the measurements in the shaded column. (1)

(ii) Explain these results. (2)

(iii) Write out a word equation for the reaction that has taken place during the demonstration. (1)

14.5 The table below contains some information about the sources and effects of greenhouse gases.

name of gas	sources of gas	percentage overall contribution to the greenhouse effect
methane		14
CFCs	aerosols, refrigerants and coolants	21
	burning forests and fossil fuels, manufacture of cement	
nitrogen oxides	breakdown of fertilisers, burning fuel in internal combustion engines	7
low level ozone	combination of nitrogen oxides with oxygen	2

The only other greenhouse gas is water vapour, which contributes 2% to the greenhouse effect.

(a) (i) Copy and complete the table, by writing into the shaded boxes the source of methane, the main greenhouse gas and the percentage contribution it makes to the greenhouse effect. (2)

(ii) Use a simple diagram to explain what is meant by a 'greenhouse gas'. (2)

(b) Suggest three possible harmful results of the greenhouse effect. (3)

(c) Burning fossil fuels also causes air pollution.

    (i)   Give the name of **two** fossil fuels. (1)

    (ii) Give the name of a gas which is the main contributor to acid rain. (1)

(d) Lakes that have been acidified by acid rain have very little remaining aquatic life. Some lakes have been treated by adding large quantities of calcium hydroxide, which quickly dissolves in the lake water.

    (i)   What effect will this have on the pH of the lake? (1)

    (ii) When the calcium hydroxide reacts with the sulphuric acid in the lake, a salt is formed. What is the name of this salt? (1)

    (iii) Write a word equation for the reaction which produces this salt. (1)

14.6 A manufacturer of model fantasy figures was interested in changing the material used to cast the models.

The manufacturer mixed two components of the resin, and then left the resin to swell. The resin needs to swell before it can be poured – it only hardens when it is baked above 200 °C. This diagram shows the changes in volume of the resin over a 30-minute period.

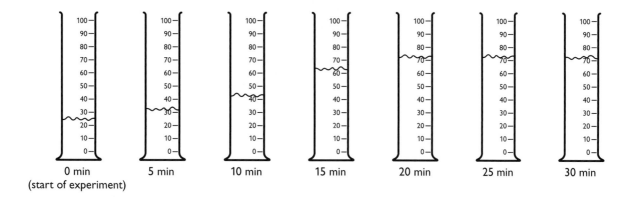

83

(a) (i) Copy and complete the table below, using the manufacturer's results. (2)

time (minutes)	volume of resin mix (cm³)
0	
5	
10	
15	
20	
25	
30	

(ii) Draw a line graph of these results on a graph grid like the one below. (3)

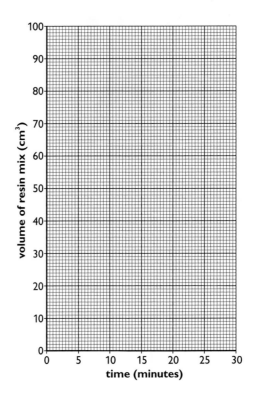

(iii) The manufacturer believed that he would get the most stable resin if he only allowed the mix to swell to two and a half times its original size. Use the graph to predict how long would he need to leave the mix to achieve this result. (1)

(b) He decided to add different quantities of a hardener to see the effect on the volume of the resin mix.

    (i)   What is the **input** (independent) **variable** in this investigation? (1)

    (ii) What is the **outcome** (dependent) **variable** in this investigation? (1)

    (iii) Give **two** other variables which the manufacturer would need to control if this were to be a fair test. (2)

(c) One feature of the hardened resin is that it does not react with air or with water. Suggest why this is important in the finished models. (1)

15: The reactions of metals

15.1 Which option best completes each of the following sentences? (5)

(a) When iron is added to lead chloride solution, lead metal is formed. This type of reaction is a

neutralisation	decomposition
displacement	combustion

(b) When iron is heated with copper oxide, the mixture glows and copper and iron oxide are formed. In this reaction

both copper and iron are oxidised	iron is oxidised and copper is reduced
both copper and iron are reduced	copper oxide is decomposed

(c) A metal which is unreactive and so would be suitable for electrical contacts is

iron	aluminium
magnesium	silver

(d) When copper carbonate is heated, the reaction which takes place is a

neutralisation	decomposition
displacement	combustion

(e) A blast furnace is a means of extracting

gold	copper
aluminium	iron

15.2 Jack was investigating the reaction between metals and hydrochloric acid. He added 20 cm³ of hydrochloric acid to each of five test tubes, and then placed equal-sized pieces of metal into four of the tubes.

iron
+
hydrochloric acid

zinc
+
hydrochloric acid

magnesium
+
hydrochloric acid

copper
+
hydrochloric acid

hydrochloric acid

(a) (i) What was the **independent** (input) **variable** in this investigation? (1)

(ii) What was the **dependent** (outcome) **variable** in this investigation? (1)

(iii) How was the outcome variable measured? (1)

(iv) Name **two** steps which Jack took to ensure that this was a fair test. (2)

(b) Arrange the four metals in order of their reactivity, with the most reactive first. (1)

(c) Jack wanted to know where gold would fit into this series, but his teacher said that gold was too expensive!

    (i) Predict the result that Jack would have obtained if he **had** been allowed to use it in his investigation. (1)

    (ii) Explain your answer. (1)

15.3 In the extraction of iron from iron ore, haematite (iron oxide) is reacted at high temperature with coke (carbon) in the presence of oxygen. The oxygen combines with the carbon to form carbon monoxide.

(a) (i) Copy and complete this word equation for the reaction between carbon monoxide and iron oxide. (3)

.... + ... $\rightarrow$ .... + carbon dioxide

    (ii) This reaction is possible because iron is **above/below** carbon in the reactivity series. Which word (above or below) is correct? (1)

(b) The cast iron produced in this way is brittle, and is usually modified in some way to make it more useful. The table below shows the percentage of carbon in four different materials.

material	percentage of carbon
cast iron	4.0
wrought iron	0.2
high carbon steel	0.8
mild steel	0.4

    (i) High carbon steel is used for some knife blades. What proportion of the carbon must be removed from cast iron to produce high carbon steel? Show your working. (2)

    (ii) The highest quality knife blades are made from stainless steel. This is made by removing most of the carbon and adding small amounts of other metals. What is the main advantage of stainless steel? (1)

(c) The graph below shows how the percentage of carbon affects the strength of the materials in the table: the strength is measured using a very complex type of force meter.

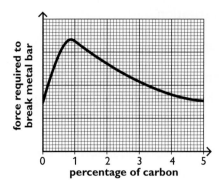

(i) What is the percentage of carbon in the material with the greatest strength? (1)

(ii) Which is the strongest material in the table? (1)

15.4 Jane added some magnesium to copper sulphate solution. She noticed that the blue solution turned paler and that the solution became warm.

(a) (i) What is this sort of reaction called? (1)

(ii) Copy and complete the equation for this reaction. (2)

magnesium + copper sulphate → .... + ...

(b) Jane decided to investigate the rise in temperature as the reaction proceeded. She repeated her experiment with magnesium, and also tried zinc and iron. She used the apparatus shown here.

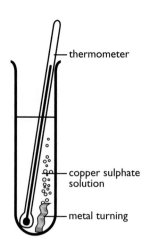

Her results are shown in the table below.

metal added to copper sulphate solution	starting temperature (°C)	final temperature (°C)	rise in temperature (°C)
magnesium	21.5	84.0	
zinc	22.0	39.5	
iron	23.0	34.5	

(i) Copy and complete the table by calculating the rise in temperature for each of the metals added. (1)

(ii) Part of the reactivity series is shown below. Copy this and add magnesium and copper in the correct positions. (1)

sodium

calcium

. . . .

aluminium

zinc

iron

lead

. . . .

Use this reactivity series to explain

(iii) why there was little difference in the results obtained for zinc and iron (1)

(iv) whether there would be a rise in temperature for any of the following mixtures

calcium and zinc sulphate (1)

lead and zinc chloride (1)

aluminium and sodium chloride (1)

15.5 Ahmed was concerned that his bike was rusting, and so tried to work out the conditions for rusting. He set up five test tubes containing iron nails as shown below.

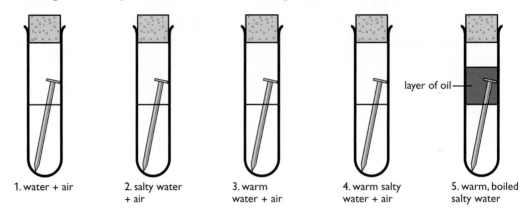

1. water + air   2. salty water + air   3. warm water + air   4. warm salty water + air   5. warm, boiled salty water

He presented his results as a bar chart, shown below.

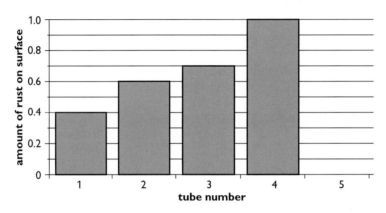

(a) (i) Copy the bar chart and add the missing bar for tube 5. (1)

Give a reason for the size of the bar. (1)

(ii) Which had the bigger effect on rusting – salt or warmth? (1)

Give a reason for your answer. (1)

(b) Ahmed set up a sixth test tube: this one contained a nail in vinegar. He saw that the iron nail reacted with the vinegar.

(i) Is vinegar acidic, alkaline or neutral? (1)

(ii) During the reaction, bubbles of gas were given off. What was this gas? (1)

(iii) If the gas could be collected, how could you test your answer? (1)

(c) Zinc is sometimes used to galvanise metal surfaces and prevent rusting.

(i) How does zinc prevent rusting? (2)

(ii) Why is galvanising not used to protect the metal on bicycle frames? (1)

15.6 The diagram shows part of the Periodic Table of Elements.

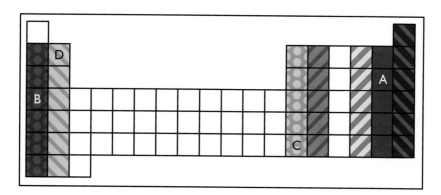

(a) (i) Which letter represents a non-metal? (1)

(ii) Which letter represents a very reactive metal? (1)

(iii) Where on the table would a less-reactive metal, such as copper or zinc, be positioned? (1)

(b) Why is silver nitrate not found in the Periodic Table? (1)

(c) An iron nail is placed into some silver nitrate solution. A reaction takes place between the iron and the silver nitrate.

(i) Copy and complete this word equation for the reaction. (3)

iron + ... → .... + ...

(ii) Copy and complete the table below to predict whether or not a reaction will take place when each of the following metals is added to the named solutions. You may use the Reactivity Table in Q. 4 to help you. (4)

Place a ✓ to show that a reaction takes place, and a ✗ if no reaction occurs.

salt solution	metal			
	copper	iron	magnesium	zinc
iron nitrate				
zinc nitrate				
calcium nitrate				

(d) Gold does not tarnish (go dull), but aluminium often does. Explain why. (1)

Physics

16: Energy sources and transformations

16.1 Which option best completes each of the following sentences? (5)

(a) Electrical energy can be converted into heat energy by

a microphone	an iron
an LED	a battery

(b) A bullet fired horizontally from a gun has been given mainly

kinetic energy	sound energy
thermal energy	chemical energy

(c) A unit used to measure energy could be a

newton	amp
degree	joule

(d) A renewable energy source which depends on naturally occurring valleys in mountainous regions is

wind	hydro
solar	wave

(e) The energy possessed by a rollercoaster car waiting at the top of the ride is

kinetic	electrical
gravitational potential	thermal

16.2 (a) This diagram shows how much heat is lost from different parts of a house.

total energy loss = 10 000 J

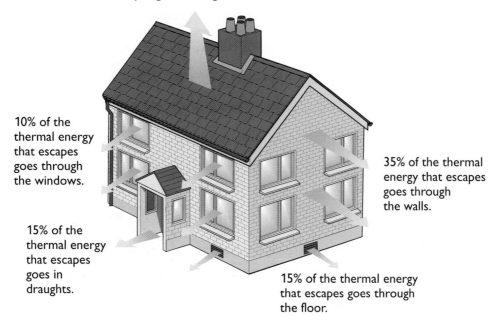

25% of the thermal energy that escapes goes through the roof.

10% of the thermal energy that escapes goes through the windows.

35% of the thermal energy that escapes goes through the walls.

15% of the thermal energy that escapes goes in draughts.

15% of the thermal energy that escapes goes through the floor.

(i) Through which part of the house is most heat lost? (1)

(ii) Cavity wall insulation can reduce heat loss through walls by 75%. If this house had the walls insulated in this way, what would be the total loss per minute from the insulated house? Show your working. (3)

(iii) Copy and complete these sentences. (3)

Foam injected into the space between walls saves heat energy because the foam is a poor .... of heat. Loft insulation works in a similar way, because the .... trapped between strands of fibreglass does not allow heat to escape. Carpets stop heat escaping though the floor, and also help to insulate against .... transfer.

(b) This diagram shows a simple draught excluder.

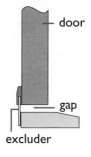

door

gap

excluder

Explain how a draught excluder can help to save heat energy. (2)

16.3 The table below lists six methods of providing energy.

method	how it works
log stove	burns dried wood to provide heat
wave turbine	uses wave energy to produce electrical energy
coal fire	burns coal to release heat
solar panel	uses light energy to provide heat
petrol generator	burns petrol to provide electrical energy
gas boiler	burns gas to provide heat

(a) (i) What is the source of energy for a solar panel? (1)

(ii) Explain how this same source of energy can drive a wind turbine. (2)

(iii) The forms of energy used in solar panels and wave turbines do not run out as they are used. What are these sources of energy described as? (1)

(b) Name **two** fossil fuels listed in the table. (2)

(c) Copy and complete these sentences. (4)

Biomass fuels (e.g. . . . .) are made because plants can carry out . . . . which converts light energy into stored . . . . energy.

A . . . . is a device that can use one form of energy to perform some work: when this occurs some energy is always lost as . . . .

16.4 An explorer has a wind up torch. This torch is powered by a steel spring, and does not use batteries.

winder

(a) The explorer winds up the spring, and as the spring unwinds, energy is transferred to a small generator. The generator then turns to provide light for the bulb in the torch.

Copy and complete these sentences to describe these energy transfers. (3)

As the spring unwinds it releases stored . . . . energy to turn the generator. The movement of the generator produces . . . . energy, and in the bulb this is converted to . . . . energy.

(b) When the explorer turns the brightness control she notices that the spring unwinds more quickly. Explain why this happens. (1)

16.5 John set up the apparatus shown in this diagram.

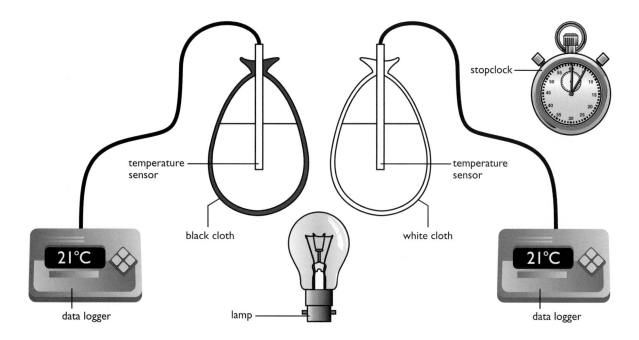

The balloons are the same colour and contain the same volume of water.

The hot lamp is kept at the same distance from the balloons.

The temperature of the water in the balloons was measured over a period of 15 minutes.

The results are shown in the table below.

time (minutes)	temperature (°C)	
	white cloth	black cloth
0	21	21
3	23	25
6	26	29
9	32	34
12	32	39
15	35	43

(a) (i) Plot these results on a grid like the one on the next page. (4)

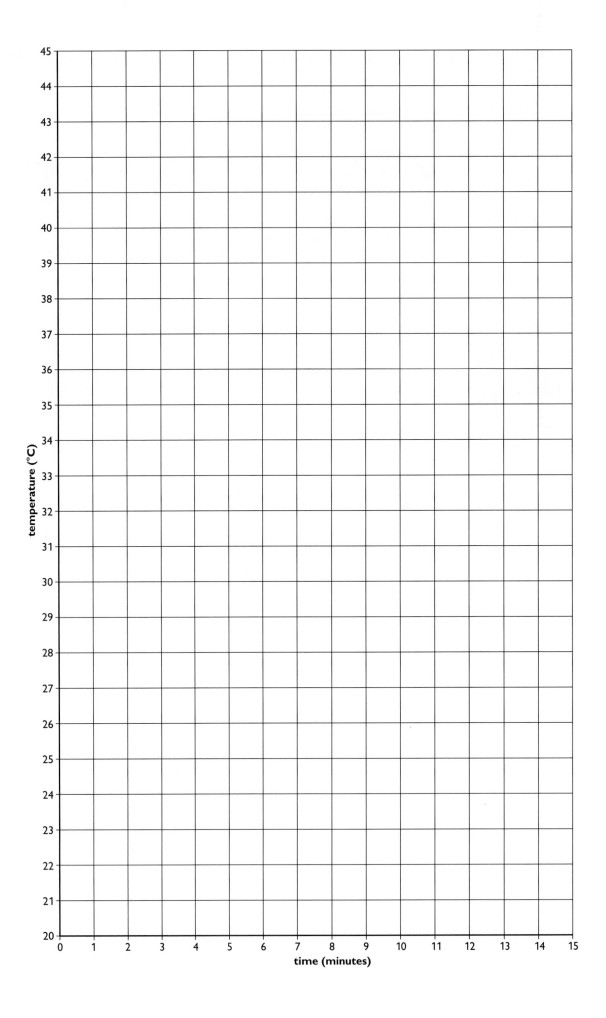

(ii)   One of the measurements appears to be incorrect. Which one? (1)

(iii) Which of the balloons allows the higher rate of heat gain? (1)

(iv)   Why is it important that the original balloons were the same colour? (1)

(b) Explain how you could adapt the apparatus to investigate whether a dull or shiny surface would be better for a solar panel. Make sure that you use the terms **independent** (input) **variable, dependent** (outcome) **variable** and controlled **variable** in your answer. (4)

16.6 (a) Copy the words in the boxes below and then draw lines to match the fossil fuels to their common uses. (2)

fossil fuels	common uses
coal	aircraft fuel
natural gas	generating electricity in power stations
petrol	cooking on camping stoves
kerosene	heating and cooking in homes
butane	fuel for cars

(b) Fossil fuels are often described as '**non-renewable**'. What does this mean? (1)

(c) (i) Much of the world's population uses biomass as a fuel. What is biomass fuel? (1)

(ii) Fossil fuels and biomass are both energy resources. What is the original source of this energy? (1)

(iii) Give **one** advantage of using fossil fuel rather than biomass as an energy resource. (1)

97

16.7 Wave (tidal) energy can be used to generate electricity. One possible method is shown in this diagram.

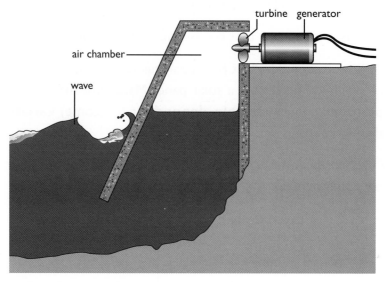

(a) Each box below shows a stage in generating electricity.

A	The turbine turns the generator

B	The moving air turns the blades of the turbine

C	The generator produces electrical energy

D	The waves move up the chamber

E	Air is pushed up the chamber by the waves

What is the correct order? (2)

(b) A group of engineers investigated how the output of energy from the wave generator depended on the speed of the waves. The results are shown in the table below.

wave speed (m/s)	0	5	10	15	20	25	30
energy output (kJ)	0	0	7	25	50	78	105

(i)   Plot this data on a grid like the one below.   (4)

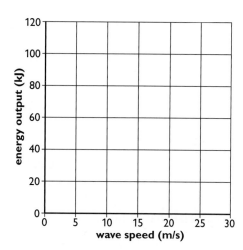

(ii) Suggest why there is no energy output if the wave speed is 5 m/s or less.   (1)

17: Electricity and energy

17.1 Which word, number or phrase best completes each of the following sentences?　　(5)

(a) In a power station a jet of steam is used to turn the blades in a

furnace	boiler
turbine	generator

(b) A mobile source of electricity is a

generator	battery
conductor	plug

(c) An example of a material that is not a good insulator is

glass	wood
plastic	graphite

(d) Electrical energy can be converted into light energy by a

solar panel	TV monitor
battery	food mixer

(e) Kinetic energy is turned into electrical energy in a

battery	petrol engine
generator	bicycle tyre

17.2 An electrical appliance changes electrical energy into another form that is useful to us. The diagrams below show what happens to the energy supplied to four appliances.

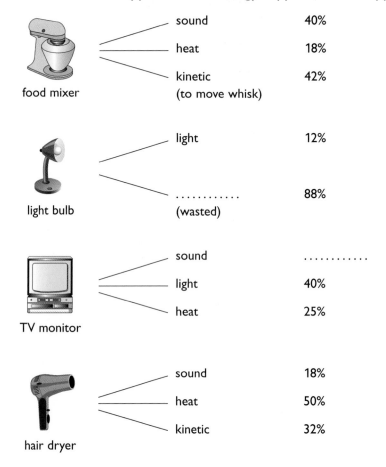

food mixer
sound 40%
heat 18%
kinetic 42%
(to move whisk)

light bulb
light 12%
.... 88%
(wasted)

TV monitor
sound ....
light 40%
heat 25%

hair dryer
sound 18%
heat 50%
kinetic 32%

(a) (i) What percentage of the energy is wasted by the food mixer? (1)

(ii) What percentage of the energy is given out as sound by the TV? (1)

(iii) Much of the energy given out by the light bulb is wasted. What sort of energy is it wasted as? (1)

(b) Two pupils were interested in saving energy in school, and decided to investigate whether all energy-saving light bulbs were equally efficient. They obtained 5 different light bulbs, all rated as 9 watts, and they set up their apparatus as shown in the diagram below:

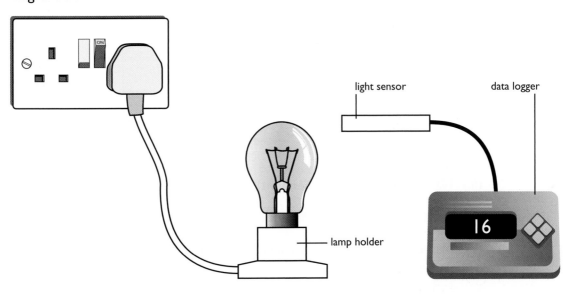

Each bulb was allowed to warm up for the same length of time, and the light sensor was always kept the same distance from the bulb. They repeated each reading three times, and they checked each other's readings on the data logger. They obtained the following results:

brand of bulb	reading 1	reading 2	reading 3	mean reading
lumo	16	18	18	
glo-bright	16	16	16	
eco-save	18	19	17	
brite-lite	21	19	20	
supa-glow	18	18	19	

(i) Calculate the mean value for each bulb. (1)

(ii) Plot these results as a bar chart on a grid like the one on the next page. (3)

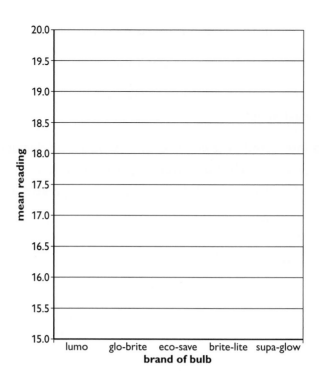

(iii) Name the **input** (independent) **variable** in their investigation. (1)

(iv) Name the **outcome** (dependent) **variable** in their investigation. (1)

(v) Name **three fixed** (controlled) **variables** that helped to make this investigation a fair test. (3)

(vi) Explain how the pupils made sure their results were reliable. (1)

(vii) Give **one** conclusion that the pupils could have drawn from their investigation. (1)

17.3 A classic car might use a dynamo as a generator. As the engine runs it uses a pulley to turn the generator. The lights on the car are directly connected to the dynamo.

(i) Copy and complete the following sentences. (5)

As the engine runs, ... energy in the petrol is changed into . . . . in the dynamo and this energy is used to provide . . . . energy carried in the wires to the lamps. The energy in the wires is changed to useful . . . . energy in the bulbs, although some is wasted as . . . .

(ii) More modern cars would have a battery between the dynamo and the lights. Explain why this is a better arrangement for the car driver. (2)

17.4 The diagram shows solar panels attached to the body of a satellite.

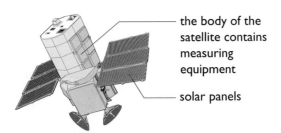

the body of the satellite contains measuring equipment

solar panels

(a) Scientists measured the output from one of these panels during one 24-hour period. Their results are shown in this diagram:

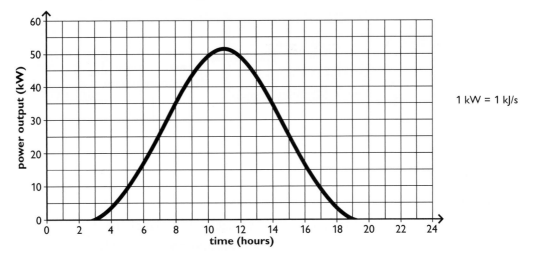

1 kW = 1 kJ/s

(i) Explain why the power output varied during the 24-hour period. (2)

(ii) The satellite used the solar panel to drive a motor. The motor needs 35 kW to run at full speed. Use the graph to work out how long the motor would be able to run at full speed. (1)

(iii) The scientists decided to improve the design so that the solar panel turns to always face the Sun. Copy the graph and draw another curve to show how the power output for the new, improved solar panel would vary during the 24-hour period. (2)

(b) Why are solar panels so useful on satellites and space stations? (1)

17.5 The diagram below shows the operation of a power station.

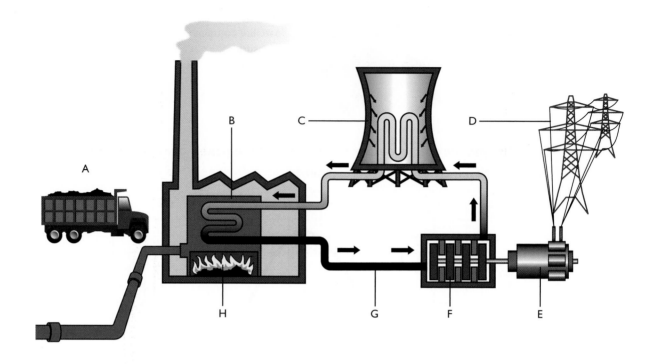

(a) Choose a word to correspond to each of the labels (A–H) on the diagram –
     not all of the words need to be used, and some could be used more than once. (5)

furnace	generator	boiler
solar panel	cooling tower	water flow
turbine	steam jet	light for power station
electricity output	fuel input	

(b) The efficiency of a power station describes how much energy is released from a
     certain mass of fuel.

     (i) The table below compares different types of power station. Work out the
          efficiency of each type of power station, giving your answers to the nearest
          whole number. (4)

type of fuel used	fuel input (tonnes)	energy output (gigajoules)	efficiency (gigajoules per tonne)
coal	1000	39 000	
oil	2000	72 000	
gas	1500	76 000	
nuclear	500	21 000	

(ii) Give **two** reasons why we would like to use less coal in power stations. (2)

(iii) Wind power is an alternative to the fuel types in the table above.
Give **one advantage** and **one disadvantage** of wind power. (2)

17.6 Electricity is a very useful form of energy.

(a) Give **two advantages** and **two disadvantages** of electricity as an energy source. (2)

(b) (i) The diagram below shows a simple electrical circuit. Explain how the apparatus could be used to compare the efficiency of **four** different materials as insulators. (2)

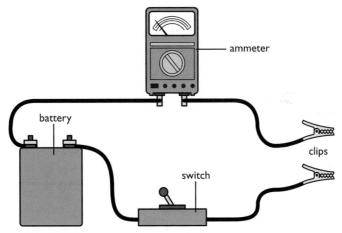

(ii) Explain **one** way in which you could make sure that this is a fair test. (1)

(iii) Name **one material** which would be a good insulator, and describe **one important use** of this material. (2)

18: Electrical circuits

18.1 Which option best completes each of the following sentences? (10)

(a) A particle with a negative charge which can flow through conductors is

an electron	a neutron
an ion	an amp

(b) A chemical source of electrical energy is a

terminal	fuse
cell	transistor

(c) The unit of electrical power is the

amp	hertz
joule	volt

(d) A device that allows the flow of current in a circuit is a

component	switch
terminal	pole

(e) The unit of electrical current is the

amp	volt
Joule	ohm

(f) A material that allows electricity to pass through it is

an insulator	a cell
a circuit	a conductor

(g) A circuit with all of the components joined in a single loop is a

parallel circuit	series circuit
conducting circuit	short circuit

(h) A component which can control the flow of a current is

a resistor	an ammeter
a cell	a motor

(i) Adding an extra cell to a series circuit which includes a lamp will make the lamp

fade	shine more brightly
shine as brightly as before	go cooler

(j) A circuit which has the same voltage across each component as across the power supply is a

parallel circuit	series circuit
conducting circuit	short circuit

18.2 (a) Give the correct name for each circuit symbol. Note that there are more names than symbols. (5)

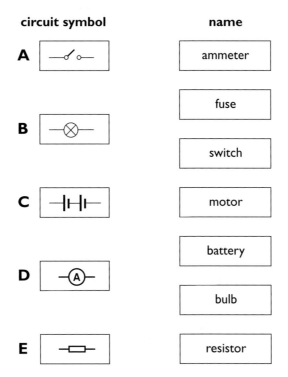

(b) James made the circuit shown in the diagram below.

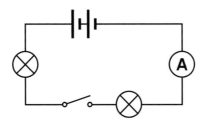

(i) What is the energy source for the circuit? (1)

(ii) Which component in the circuit is used to measure the current flow? (1)

(iii) Re-draw the circuit so that it becomes a parallel circuit. (2)

(c) Which is the most commonly used metal to make the wires in electric circuits? (1)

18.3 (a) A teacher was demonstrating circuits to her pupils. She built this circuit.

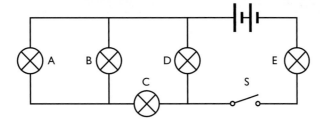

She closed the switch and all of the bulbs came on. One of the bulbs then failed, and all of the bulbs went out. Which one of the bulbs must have failed? (1)

(b) The teacher then built a second circuit. She included a metal pencil sharpener and a plastic pencil sharpener in different parts of the circuit.

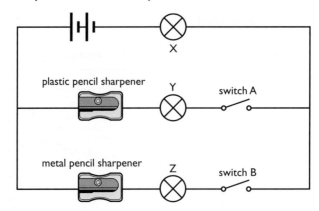

Copy and complete the table below to show which bulbs in this circuit will be **on** and which will be **off** when the switches are open or closed. (2)

switch A	switch B	bulb X	bulb Y	bulb Z
open	open	off	off	off
closed	open			
open	closed			

(c) Finally the teacher built this circuit, using a battery, three bulbs and four ammeters.

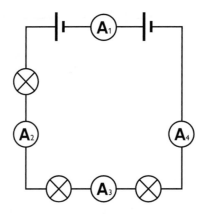

The current reading at ammeter A₁ was 0.6 amps. Which set of readings for the other ammeters, shown in the table below, is correct? (1)

reading on A₂	reading on A₃	reading on A₄
0.2	0.2	0.2
0.3	0.0	0.3
0.6	0.6	0.6

18.4 (a) The diagram below shows the parts of a cycle lamp.

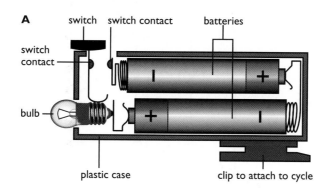

(i)   Anna closed the switch. Why did this light the lamp?   (1)

(ii) Use the correct symbols to draw a circuit diagram for the lamp.   (3)

(b) Jamie borrowed the cycle lamp. The lamp would not light even when the switch was closed. The two diagrams show possible reasons for this.

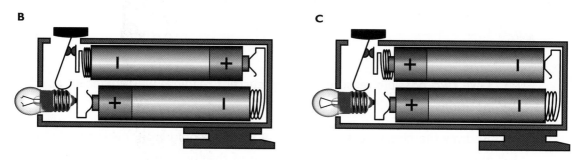

In each case, **B** and **C**, describe and explain what needs to be done to get the lamp to light.   (4)

18.5 Janet and Imran were asked whether the thickness or the length of a piece of wire is more important in affecting its resistance. They were supplied with the following equipment:

battery	roll of thin copper wire
switch	roll of thin steel wire
ammeter	ruler with millimetre markings
roll of thick copper wire	

(a) Draw a circuit which they could use in their investigation.   (2)

(b) For their investigation to be a fair test, identify the

(i)   **input** (independent) **variable**   (1)

(ii) **outcome** (dependent) **variable**   (1)

(iii) **fixed** (controlled) **variables**   (2)

(c) How could they try to make sure that their results were reliable?   (1)

18.6 A student built the following circuit. He had only one ammeter, so he placed it first at A_1, then at A_2, then at A_3.

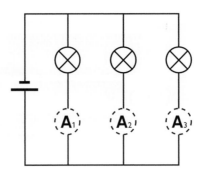

The table below shows the results he obtained when he measured the current in the different positions.

ammeter at position	measured current (amps)
A_1	0.26
A_2	0.29
A_3	0.27

(a) Give **two** possible reasons why the current readings were different at different positions. (2)

(b) Redraw the circuit to show how the student could have investigated whether the total current would equal the sum of the three values he obtained at A_1, A_2 and A_3. (1)

(c) The student left the circuit set up as in (b). He used a datalogger to measure the current every hour. The next day the bulbs were dim. Draw a sketch graph showing how the current would change with time. Be sure to include the correct labels on the axes, and show the shape of the graph you would expect to obtain. (2)

18.7 The diagram shows a room heater used to warm up the gym on cold mornings!

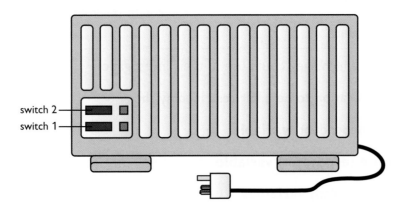

The school electrician had a diagram which showed the circuit for the heater.

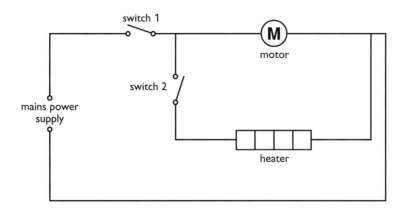

(a) (i) Which combination of switches must be closed for the heater to work? (1)

(ii) Is it possible to have the heater on when the blower motor is switched off?
Explain your answer. (1)

(iii) The heater and the motor are both on. A wire in the heater breaks.
What effect will this have on the blower motor? (1)

(b) The school electrician was asked to check the lighting in the corridor leading to
the gym. The corridor has a switch at each end and one light bulb in the middle.
The circuit diagram below shows how they are connected.

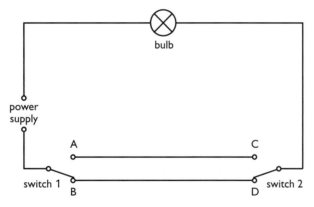

Copy and complete the table below to show the effect of the different possible
switch positions. (1)

position of switch 1	position of switch 2	bulb on or off?
B	D	
A	D	
A	C	

(c) The electrician decides to change the circuit so that there is a bulb at each end of the corridor.

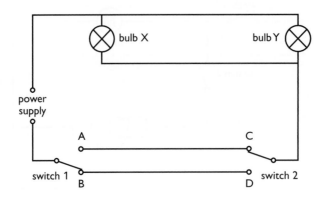

(i) With the switches as shown in the diagram which bulbs, if any, are on? (1)

(ii) The switches are arranged so that both bulbs are on. Bulb X breaks.
What, if anything, happens to bulb Y? (1)

19: Magnetic fields and electromagnetism

19.1 Which option best completes each of the following sentences? (5)

(a) The ends of a magnet are called

tips	poles
terminals	fields

(b) An example of a metal that is not magnetic is

iron	nickel
copper	cobalt

(c) A magnetic field has

force but no direction	both force and direction
direction but no force	neither force nor direction

(d) An electromagnet can be made stronger by reducing the

diameter of the wire	resistance of the wire
current	number of turns in the coil

(e) The coil of wire making up part of an electromagnet is the

solenoid	turning
core	relay

19.2 (a) David is investigating the properties of magnets, and wants to find a magnetic material. He has three pieces of metal – one is made of steel, one is made of copper and one is a magnet. He does not know which piece is which, but marks each one with a letter (X, Y or Z) and then uses a bar magnet to try to identify them.

He places the marked end of each piece of metal next to each pole of the bar magnet, and writes down what happens in a table of results. Copy and complete this table of results. (3)

test	result	conclusion
X S N	attract	metal X is
X N S	attract	....
Y S N	....	metal Y is
Y N S	attract	....
Z S N	....	metal Z is
Z N S	nothing happens	....

113

(b) David took the piece of metal which was magnetic and laid it beneath a piece of card. He then sprinkled iron filings onto the card. Draw a diagram showing the pattern he would have seen. (2)

(c) David then took a small compass and placed it near to the magnet. Draw a diagram to show what would have happened to the compass. (1)

(d) Copy and complete this paragraph. (4)

When an unmagnetised iron nail is put into a .... it becomes magnetised. The South-seeking pole of this nail will be .... to the .... pole of a bar magnet, but will be .... by the South pole of the magnet.

19.3 The end of morning school is normally signalled by ringing an electric bell. The diagram shows the circuit for this bell.

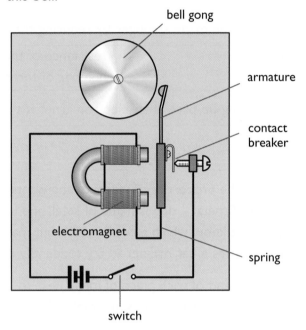

(a) The bell is normally silent (good idea during lessons!). Explain why. (2)

(b) Write out, in the correct order, what happens to make the bell ring. (5)

114

19.4 A current flowing through a coiled wire acts like a magnet. The strength of this electromagnetic field can be increased by placing a core inside the coiled wire. A pupil decided to investigate the effect of the core material on the strength of the electromagnetic field. She used this apparatus.

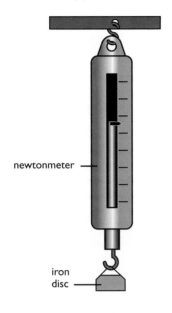

newtonmeter

iron disc

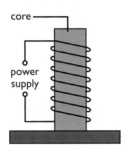

core

power supply

(a) Name three factors which should be kept constant to keep this as a fair test. (3)

(b) The pupil obtained the following results.

material in core	reading on newtonmeter (N)
iron (no current)	1.0
current on (no core)	1.4
iron	1.8
glass	
steel	1.6

(i) Explain why the reading on the newtonmeter increases when a current passes through the coil. (2)

(ii) Suggest the likely value for the reading with glass as the core. (1)

19.5 A reed switch is a small relay used in electronic circuits. It has thin metal contacts inside a glass tube.

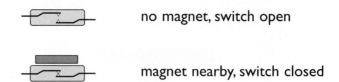

no magnet, switch open

magnet nearby, switch closed

(a) Jane set up the circuit shown below.

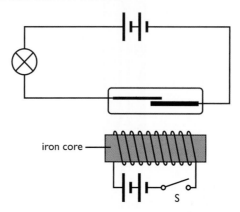

iron core

S

(i) She closed switch S but the lamp did not light. She knew that all of the connections had been made properly, and that the bulb was not broken. Explain why the lamp might not have lit. (2)

(ii) Suggest **two** things Jane could do to the electromagnet to overcome this problem. (2)

(b) A security expert wanted to use a normally-closed (NC) reed switch in a battery-operated intruder alarm. He thought he could use the circuit below.

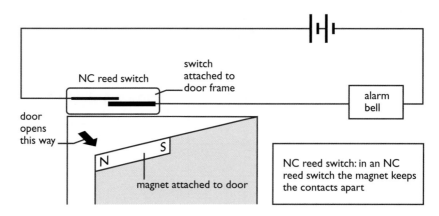

NC reed switch

switch attached to door frame

alarm bell

door opens this way

N   S

magnet attached to door

NC reed switch: in an NC reed switch the magnet keeps the contacts apart

Explain how opening the door will set off the intruder alarm. (2)

19.6 Saira used a sensor to measure the strength of an electromagnet. She placed the sensor 50 mm from the electromagnet and increased the current in the coil. She then turned the current down to zero, moved the sensor to 100 mm from the electromagnet, and repeated the experiment.

The results are shown in the table opposite.

sensor at 50 mm distance	
current (amps)	sensor reading (N)
0.5	0.35
1.0	0.68
1.5	1.00
2.0	1.30
2.5	1.50

sensor at 100 mm distance	
current (amps)	sensor reading (N)
0.5	0.15
1.0	0.30
1.5	0.45
2.0	0.55
2.5	0.60

(a)   Draw a graph of these results on a grid like the one below.   (5)

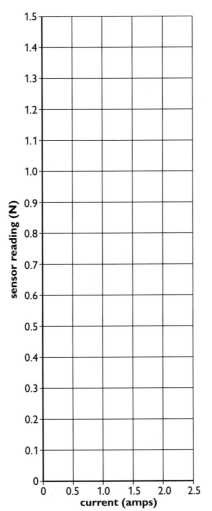

(b) (i) How did the size of the current in the coil affect the strength of the electromagnet? (1)

   (ii) Suggest **two** other ways that Saira could have altered the strength of the electromagnet. (2)

(c) An electromagnet can be used at a railway crossing barrier.

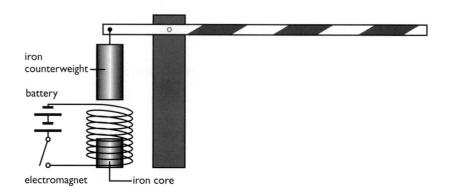

Explain how the electromagnet can be used to raise the barrier. (2)

19.7 Andy made two electromagnets as shown below. The strength of the electromagnet was measured by how many paper clips could be picked up.

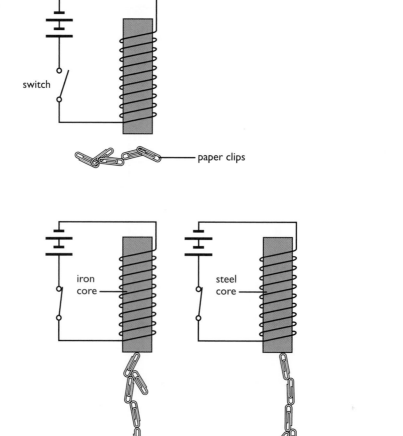

(a) (i) How can you tell that the strength of both electromagnets is the same? (1)

(ii) When the switches are opened the paper clips fall from the iron core but not from the steel core. Why is iron, rather than steel, used for the core of an electromagnet? (1)

(b) The diagram below shows an electromagnet used in a scrapyard for separating different metals.

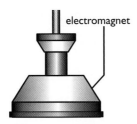

pile of metal:
mixed iron/steel/aluminium

Explain how the electromagnet can separate the valuable aluminium from the less valuable steel. (2)

(c) Some parts of the electromagnet crane are protected by circuit breakers.
These automatically switch off a circuit if the current is too high. This diagram shows a simple circuit breaker.

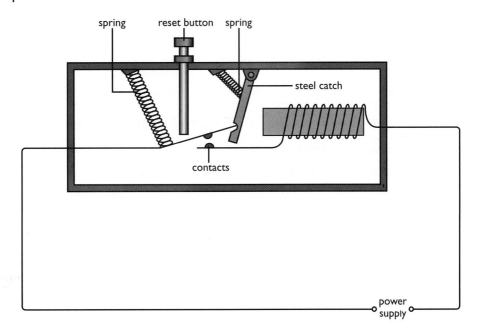

(i) Explain why the current is cut off by this circuit breaker if it is larger than a certain value. (2)

(ii) Give **one** advantage of this type of circuit breaker compared with a simple electrical fuse. (1)

20: Heat and energy

20.1 Which word, phrase or number best completes the following sentences? (10)

(a) A metal fork feels colder than a plastic one because we lose more heat to it by

radiation	convection
conduction	evaporation

(b) A temperature scale that starts at 0 and has 373 as the boiling point of pure water is the

Celsius scale	Kelvin scale
Fahrenheit scale	Centigrade scale

(c) The energy possessed by particles as a result of their movement is

thermal energy	gravitational energy
kinetic energy	light energy

(d) The correct unit of heat energy is the

degree Celsius	joule
watt	kelvin

(e) Heat travelling from a bonfire reaches us mainly by

radiation	convection
conduction	evaporation

(f) Normal body temperature in a human is

36.9 °F	36.9 °C
95 °F	273 K

(g) An elephant sprays water onto its skin to try to lose heat by

radiation	convection
conduction	evaporation

(h) Dolphins and porpoises have a thick layer of blubber beneath their skin because it is

a good thermal insulator
a good thermal conductor
soft enough to give them the right shape for swimming
an excellent food for their young

(i) Opening the door on a cold night allows heat to leave the room by

radiation	convection
conduction	evaporation

(j) The efficiency of a device compares

heat lost with heat gained
energy input with heat output
useful energy output with energy input
rise in temperature with heating time

20.2 Foxes can keep cool by losing heat from their ears because blood flows close to the skin there. This diagram shows two foxes from different parts of the world.

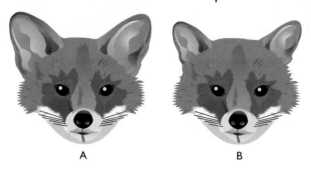

A   B

(a) (i) Which fox lives in Greenland, and which one lives in Kenya? Give a reason for your answer. (2)

   (ii) When the fox is hot after hunting, it sometimes lies down with its belly on cool soil. How does this behaviour help it to lose heat? (1)

(b) Jamie decided to investigate heat loss by the foxes. He used tin cans with strips of metal attached as models for the foxes.

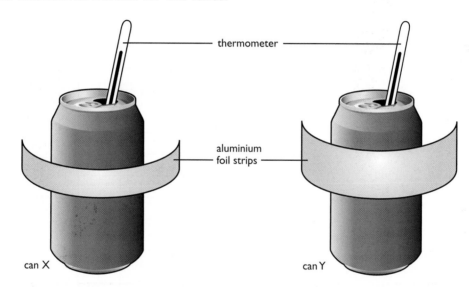

He carefully filled the two cans with 300 cm³ of very hot water, and then used a thermometer to measure the temperature of the water in the can every 2 minutes, for 10 minutes.

The results are shown in this table.

time (minutes)	temperature in can **X** (°C)	temperature in can **Y** (°C)
0	65	65
2	61	59
4	58	54
6	55	49
8	53	45
10	51	41

(i)   Give **two** ways in which Jamie made this a fair test. (2)

(ii) Plot the results on a graph grid like the one below. Label the axes carefully and draw lines of best fit. (4)

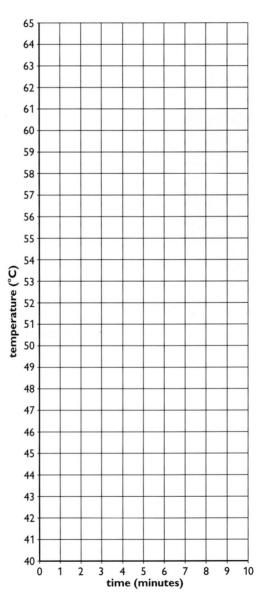

(iii) Do the results support your answer to (a) (i)? Explain your reason for making this choice. (2)

(c) Jamie had watched a wildlife film, and he noticed that the foxes often flattened their ears when they were in cold places. He altered his apparatus so that the strips of metal were flat against the cans.

flaps folded around can

(i) What do you think he will have observed as he measured the temperatures? (1)

(ii) Jamie's teacher said that this final experiment wasn't really a fair test. Explain why. (2)

20.3 (a) In a brass rod the particles vibrate. If one end of the rod is heated, heat is transferred to the other end of the rod.

(i) What is this form of heat transfer called? (1)

(ii) Use your understanding of particles to explain **how** this process takes place. (1)

(b) An electric immersion heater can be used to raise the temperature of the water in a tropical aquarium. The water next to the heater becomes warm.

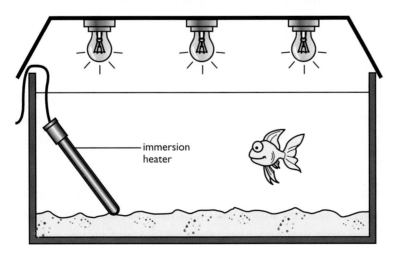

immersion heater

(i) Copy the diagram and then draw arrows on, and add labels to explain how heat is transferred to other parts of the aquarium. (2)

(ii) Why can heat not be transferred in this way in the brass rod? (1)

(iii) The lamps above the aquarium also heat the water in the tank. What is the name of the process which transfers heat from the hot lamps in this way? (1)

(c) Some of the particles of water have enough kinetic energy to escape from the surface. This process goes on even when the water temperature is well below boiling point.

(i) What is this process called? (1)

(ii) What effect will this have on the temperature of the water left in the aquarium? (1)

(iii) Explain your answer. (1)

20.4 (a) Some people are worried that if they eat too much fat they will become overweight. Humans use fat obtained from food as a long-term store of energy. The energy content of a fatty food can be investigated using the apparatus shown below:

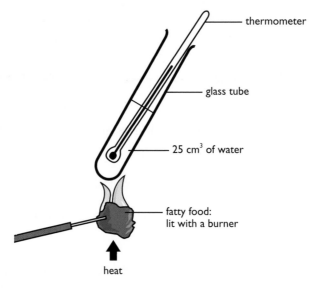

(i) What is the **input** (independent) **variable** in this experiment? (1)

(ii) What is the **outcome** (dependent) **variable**? (1)

(iii) Give **two** factors which should be kept constant to keep this a fair test. (2)

(iv) 4.2 J of energy will raise the temperature of 1 cm³ of water by 1 °C. 1 g of fat contains 38 500 J of energy. Calculate the rise in temperature of 25 cm³ of water if 0.2 g of fat is burned in this way. Show your working, and give your answer to the nearest whole number. (3)

(v) In the actual experiment the temperature rise was much less than expected. The science teacher suggested that this might be due to heat losses. Give **two** ways in which heat might be lost and so not heat up the water. (2)

(b) (i) Fat is stored beneath the skin, where it forms part of the body's energy store. Give another function of the layers of fat. (1)

(ii) Small babies lose heat much more quickly than their parents. What does this suggest about their layers of fat? (1)

(iii) What can parents do to protect their babies against heat loss? (1)

20.5 The diagrams show a shot putter at an athletics championships. The stages in the shot putt are labelled A, B, C, D and E.

Copy and complete the following sentences. (4)

(i) The energy for lifting the shot had been stored as .... energy in the .... of the man's arms. The energy is released from this store by the process of ...., which goes on more efficiently if the gas .... is present.

(ii) At stage C, the energy in the shot is stored as (1)

| chemical energy | gravitational potential energy |
| thermal energy | kinetic energy |

(iii) At stage D, as the shot flies through the air it possesses both .... energy and .... energy. (2)

(iv) At stage E, as the shot hits the ground, the energy was transferred from .... to .... energy. (2)

125

21: The Earth and the Solar System

21.1 Which option best completes each of the following sentences? (10)

(a) On the Moon, gravity exerts a force of 1.6 N on 1 kg. An object that has a weight of 240 N on the Moon, has a mass of

| 400 kg | 150 kg | 160 kg | 240 kg |

(b) An eclipse of the Moon occurs when

the Sun lies between the Earth and the Moon
the Moon lies between the Sun and the Earth
the Moon is waning
the Earth lies between the Sun and the Moon

(c) The Sun is a

| constellation | star |
| galaxy | planet |

(d) The time taken for the Moon to complete one orbit of the Earth is a

| year | lunar month |
| day | season |

(e) We are sometimes able to see planets because

| they are luminous | asteroids collide with the planet's surface |
| they reflect light from the Moon | they reflect light from the Sun |

(f) Gravity on the Moon is less than on the Earth because

the Moon is smaller than the Earth
the Moon is further away from the Sun
objects on the Moon have less mass than on the Earth
the Moon is rotating quicker

(g) The planet with an orbit closest to the orbit of the Earth is

| Mars | Mercury |
| Jupiter | Venus |

(h) Compared with sound, light travels

| much slower | much faster |
| at the same speed | slightly faster |

(i) The most commonly used communications satellites are

| in polar orbit | in low Earth orbit |
| geostationary | in high elliptical orbit |

(j) Distances in space are so great that they are measured in

| millions of kilometres | light years |
| parsecs | galactic gigametres |

21.2 The diagram below shows the positions of the Earth, Moon and Sun during a lunar eclipse.

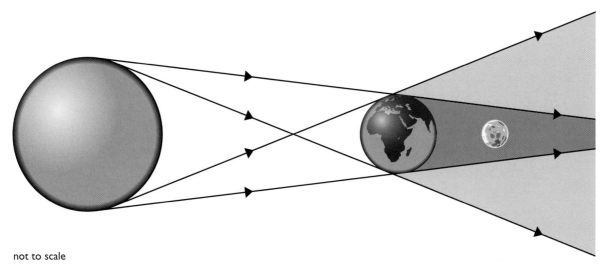

not to scale

(a) Redraw the diagram and add labels to **Sun**, **Moon**, **Earth** and **partial shadow**. (2)

(b) A solar eclipse can upset the singing patterns of birds. Why do you think this is? (1)

(c) Draw a second diagram showing the position of the Sun, Moon, Earth and complete shadow (umbra) during a solar eclipse. Label your diagram. (3)

(d) The Sarus Cycle is a regular cycle of solar eclipses. The table shows the dates of some eclipses in this cycle.

eclipse	date
A	9th July 1945
B	20th July 1963
C	
D	11th August 1999

Calculate the date of eclipse C. (2)

21.3 Copy and complete the following sentences. (6)

We are able to see stars because they are . . . . Many stars seem to be arranged in patterns called . . . . and there may be several of these in a single . . . . The stars may be a great distance from the Earth and may only be visible with an instrument called a . . . . and we have to measure distances in . . . . All the planets, stars, gases and dust together make up the . . . .

21.4 The diagram shows a satellite in orbit around the Earth.

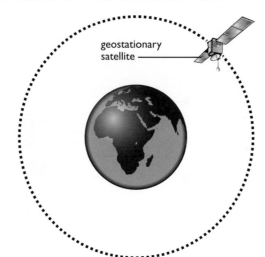

geostationary
satellite

not to scale

(a) Copy the diagram and draw dots and labels to show how a transmitter and
receiver would allow a football match to be seen in a different country.
Do not worry too much about drawing the countries accurately. (2)

(b) (i) Why is it important for the satellite to remain in the same position above
the Earth? (1)

(ii) How long does one complete orbit of the satellite take? (1)

(iii) What is the force which keeps the satellite in position above the Earth? (1)

(iv) Explain why the Global Positioning System depends on more than
one satellite. (2)

(c) Name **one** natural satellite of the Earth, and **one** of the Sun. (2)

21.5 Copy the words in the boxes below and then draw lines to match each observation
to the correct explanation. (5)

observation   **explanation**

| one year on Earth is 365 days |

| the Earth's axis is tilted |

| at the Equator, there are 12 hours of light and 12 hours of darkness |

| the Moon orbits the Earth |

| in Britain there are four seasons in the year |

| the Earth orbits the Sun |

| there is a new Moon every month |

| the Earth is a sphere |

| a ship sailing away from land goes out of sight |

| the Earth rotates on its axis |

21.6 This diagram shows a model of the solar system.

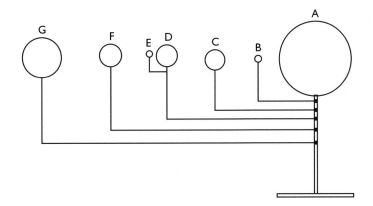

(a) Give the letter that is used to label

   (i)   the model Earth   (1)

   (ii) the model planet with the highest surface temperature   (1)

   (iii) a star   (1)

   (iv) the model planet with the highest gravity   (1)

(b) Spacecraft have allowed humans to stand on the surface of the Moon. This diagram
    shows an astronaut standing at four different positions on the Moon.

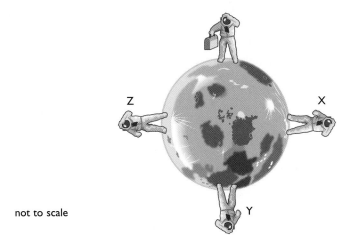

not to scale

   (i)   Copy the diagram and draw an arrow at each of the four positions to show
         the direction of the force of the Moon's gravity on the astronaut.   (1)

   (ii) The astronaut is holding a bag for collecting samples on a chain. Draw the
         position of the bag in positions X, Y and Z.   (1)

(c) The diagram shows that the Earth orbits the Sun.

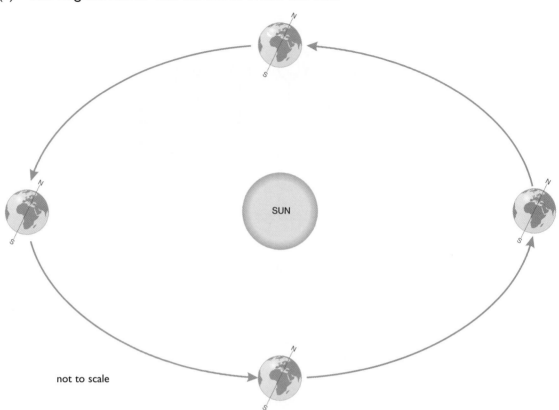

not to scale

(i) Explain why the Earth orbits the Sun. (2)

(ii) How long does it take for the Earth to orbit the Sun once? (1)

(iii) Light travels at 300 000 km per second. The Sun is 149 million km from the Earth. How long does light take to reach the Earth from the Sun? Show your working. (2)

21.7 The diagram shows our solar system.

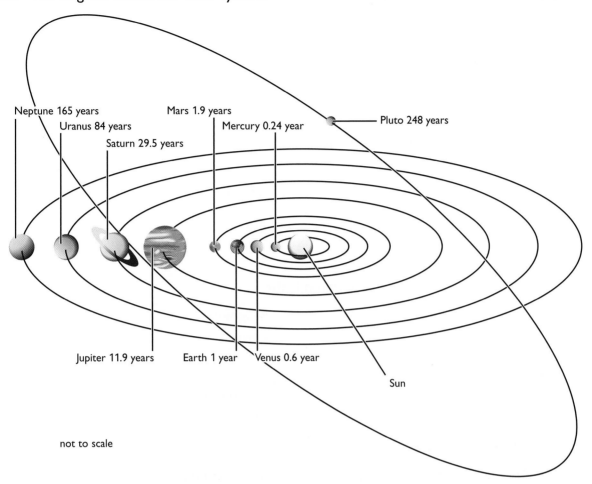

Neptune 165 years
Uranus 84 years
Saturn 29.5 years
Mars 1.9 years
Mercury 0.24 year
Pluto 248 years
Jupiter 11.9 years
Earth 1 year
Venus 0.6 year
Sun

not to scale

(a) (i) What evidence from the diagram supports the idea that Pluto is **not** a planet? (1)

(ii) The Hubble telescope has allowed astronomers to observe an object called Charon which orbits Pluto. How does this support the idea that Pluto **is** a planet? (1)

(b) The diagram below shows the path of a comet around the Sun.

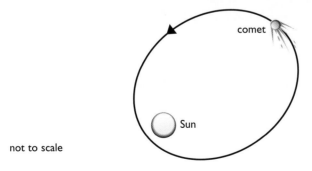

comet
Sun
not to scale

(i) Copy the diagram and mark with a letter X the point at which the comet is moving most quickly, and with a letter Y the point at which the comet is travelling most slowly. (1)

(ii) Explain your answer. (1)

22: Forces and linear motion

22.1 Which option best completes each of the following sentences? (5)

(a) A metal which has a density of 4 g per cm^3 and a mass of 30 g will have a volume of

10.0 cm^3	15.0 cm^3
30.0 cm^3	7.5 cm^3

(b) Speed can be calculated from the formula Speed =

time × distance	$\dfrac{time}{distance}$
$\dfrac{distance}{time}$	$\dfrac{distance}{time^2}$

(c) The unit in which force is measured is the

joule	kilogram
watt	newton

(d) The speed of a moving object will remain the same if

it is in a vacuum	all forces on it are balanced
there is no gravity acting on it	there is a constant force on it

(e) Forces always have

size only	direction only
a size and a direction	no value when an object is not moving

22.2 A drag racing car was being tested over a distance of 500 m. The digital stopwatch used to measure the time taken can measure to 0.01 of a second. The car was tested six times – three times in each direction.

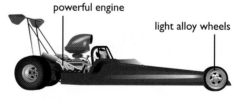

powerful engine

light alloy wheels

(a) The results of the timing are shown in the table below.

run number	time taken (seconds)
1	6.02
2	6.23
3	6.00
4	6.19
5	8.24
6	6.21

(i) Which run was an anomalous result? (1)

(ii) If the anomalous result is ignored, calculate the mean value for the time taken for the run. (1)

(iii) How does a mean value make the results more reliable? (1)

(b) (i) What is the formula used to calculate the speed of the car? (1)

(ii) Calculate the average speed of the car. Show your working, and give your answer to one decimal place. (2)

(c) Give **one** reason why the results for runs 2, 4 and 6 were higher than those for runs 1 and 3, other than that the car travelled faster in one direction. (1)

22.3 The diagram shows a submarine moving on the surface of the sea.

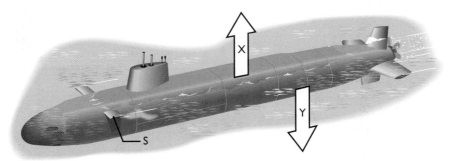

(a) Two of the forces acting on the submarine are marked X and Y. Identify these forces. (2)

(b) The submarine now starts to move away from the dock. Name the **two** forces that resist the movement of the submarine when it is moving quickly. (2)

(c) The commander of the submarine now decides that the vessel should dive below the surface. To do this he must alter the angle of the stabilisers labelled S. Draw a sketch of the submarine and mark on the position of the stabiliser as the submarine dives beneath the surface. (1)

22.4 Valentino Rossi is a champion motorcyclist. His team work on his motorcycle to improve its performance by adding the fairing.

fairing   leather clothing

(a) (i) How does the fairing help to improve the speed of the motorcycle? (1)

(ii) The motorcycle does not slide off at the bends because of a force between the tyres and the track surface. What is the name of this force? (1)

(iii) If the motorcyclist falls from the machine it is important that he slides along the track and slowly comes to a halt. What important property of his leather suit helps this? (1)

(b) Valentino Rossi's engineers measured the distance travelled by his motorcycle along part of the straight. They obtained these results:

time (seconds)	distance travelled (m)
0	0
1	200
2	399
3	599
4	801
5	1000
6	1201
7	1400
8	1600

(i) Plot these results on a grid like the one below. (3)

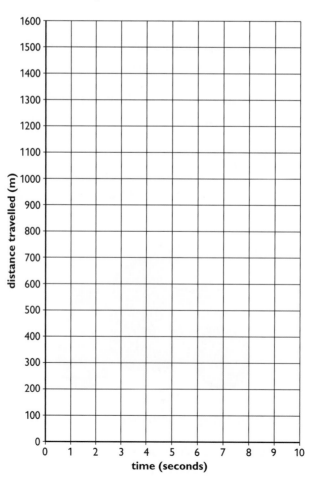

(ii) What was the average speed, in metres per second, during this period? (1)

(iii) From the graph, how far had the motorcycle travelled after 3.5 s? (1)

(iv) How far did the motorcycle travel between 4.5 and 7.5 s? (1)

(v) If the motorcycle continues at this speed, how long would it take to cover 2.5 km? (1)

22.5 Karen wanted to investigate the relationship between mass and weight. She used a forcemeter to do this, and obtained the following results:

mass (g)	weight (N)
100	1.0
200	2.0
300	3.0
400	4.4
550	5.5
660	6.6

(a) (i) One of the results does not seem to fit the pattern of the other results. Which is the anomalous result? (1)

(ii) Use the information in this table to predict

the mass of an object weighing 4.3 N

the weight of an object of mass 240 g (2)

(b) Copy and complete these sentences. (4)

Weight is a force caused by . . . . acting on an object.
. . . . is not a force, and depends on the . . . .
and . . . . of particles in an object.

(c) An astronaut working on the space shuttle can take a space walk, and can move using four small jet motors attached to his space suit. This diagram shows the size and direction of four forces acting on the astronaut.

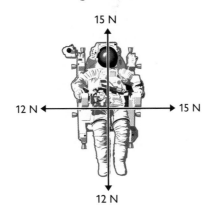

(i) The astronaut can move even though the forces produced by the jets are small. Explain why. (2)

(ii) Sketch a picture of the astronaut and add an arrow to show the direction in which he would move. (1)

22.6 Rockets can be used to take astronauts into space. The diagram shows such a rocket shortly after take off.

(a) The rocket is powered by burning a fuel load of liquid hydrogen and oxygen.

(i) Explain why the fuel is transported as liquids rather than as gases. (2)

(ii) Explain why oxygen is needed to burn the fuel, although vehicles do not need liquid oxygen when they transport the rockets around the launch sites on Earth. (1)

(b) (i) On the diagram above, what are the two forces represented by the two arrows alongside the rocket? (2)

(ii) The graph below shows how the upward force and the weight of the rocket (including fuel) change during the first 40 seconds after ignition.

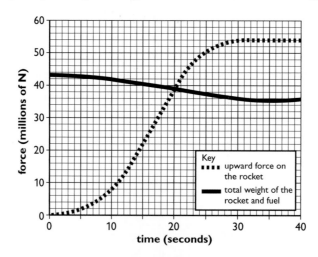

Use the graph to explain why the rocket cannot take off before 20 seconds have passed. (1)

(iii) What is the resultant force on the rocket after 30 seconds? (1)

(iv) Why does the total weight of the shuttle decrease during the first
30 seconds? (1)

22.7 During the school cross-country race, the time taken by one of the boys was measured at different distances around the course. The results are shown in the graph below.

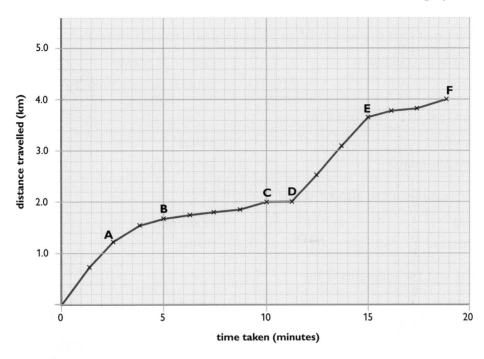

(a) (i) How long did the runner take to complete the course? (1)

(ii) At which point did the boy need to stop and tie his shoelace? (1)

(iii) Which part of the graph suggests that he was running up a steep hill? (1)

(iv) What was the average speed over the whole journey? Give your answer
in km per hour, and to 1 decimal place. Show your working. (2)

(b) (i) Why did the boy wear trainers with ridges and spikes in the soles? (1)

(ii) Copy and complete the following sentence. (3)

During the race, the boy's muscles converted . . . .
energy into . . . . energy (and also into . . . .
energy, which made him sweat).

23: Friction and motion

23.1 Which option best completes each of the following sentences? (5)

(a) The strength of the turning effect of a force is a

| movement | leverage |
| moment | rotator |

(b) The point that the weight of an object appears to pass through is the

| centre of stability | centre of gravity |
| pivot | counterbalance point |

(c) The unit of pressure is the

| newton | pascal |
| newton-metre | foot-pound |

(d) Air resistance can also be called

| drag | hindrance |
| pressure | thrust |

(e) The unit for moments is the

| newton | pascal |
| newton-metre | newton per m² |

23.2 A farmer tried to pull out a tree stump by pulling with a rope.

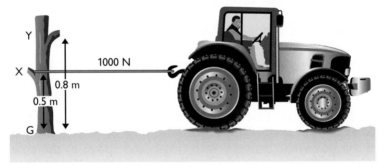

not to scale

(a) (i) The farmer attached a rope to the branch at point X, 0.5 m above the ground. He pulled with a force of 1000 N. Calculate the turning moment about the pivot point G. (2)

(ii) The farmer then attached a rope to branch Y, 0.8m above the ground. What horizontal force would produce the same turning moment as before? (1)

(b) The tyres on the farmer's tractor have many grooves and ridges. Explain why this is important when working in a muddy field. (1)

(c) (i) Once the tree stump has been pulled out of the ground, the farmer decides to chop it up with an axe. The edge of the blade is sharpened so that it is very narrow. Explain why. (1)

(ii) The blade of the axe has an area of 1.2 cm², and the farmer can apply a force of 600 N. What pressure can the farmer exert on the tree? (Remember that there are 10 000 cm² in 1 m²). Show your working. (2)

23.3 Scientists have observed that in some parts of the world polar bears are interbreeding with grizzly bears. The hybrid animal is called a grolar bear! Look at this drawing of a polar bear.

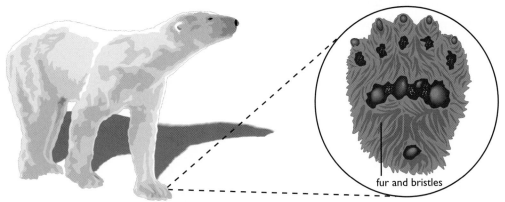

fur and bristles

(a) (i) One difference between the two types of bear is that the true polar bear has much broader feet than the grizzly bear. How could these broad feet help the polar bear in its natural habitat, where it must walk across snowfields? (2)

(ii) There is also another difference in the feet of the polar bear and the grizzly. The polar has many hairs on the soles of its feet, but the grizzly does not. Some of these hairs are short (like bristles), and some are more like fur. What are the advantages to the polar bear, in its natural habitat, of the **bristles** and of the **fur-like** hairs? (2)

(b) Copy and complete the following sentences. (2)

Inuit hunters who look for the polar bears rub fat and oil onto the runners of their sledges. The oil acts as a . . . . to reduce . . . . between the runners and the ice.

23.4 The diagram shows a Siamang (a type of gibbon), hanging on a vine in a forest.

vine

2 M

(a) (i) Would an arrow showing the direction of the Siamang's weight point up or down? (1)

(ii) Would an arrow showing the direction of the force of the vine on the Siamang point up or down? (1)

(b) The Siamang can just reach the end of a branch of another tree. The branch is 2 m long, and the Siamang has a mass of 12 kg. Calculate the turning moment applied when the Siamang grabs the branch and lets go of the vine. Show your working. (2)

(c) The Siamang is able to bite into the fruit because it has strong jaws. The diagram below shows how the animal uses its jaws to bite the fruit.

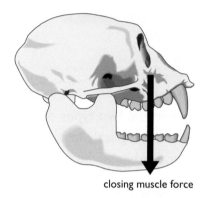

closing muscle force

(i) The jaws work because there is a pivot in them. Draw two lines to represent the upper and lower jaws shown in the diagram, and label the pivot. (1)

(ii) The Siamang pulls the fruit it is eating close to the pivot. Explain why this makes it easier to break open the fruit. (2)

23.5 Jack and Billy were going to build a model railway layout. They thought that they could glue a baseboard onto an old desk, even though the baseboard would overlap the desk by 50 cm. Their teacher thought the board would sag, and might even break, if they added any heavy items to it, and suggested that they carry out a test first. The diagram below shows the apparatus they used for their test.

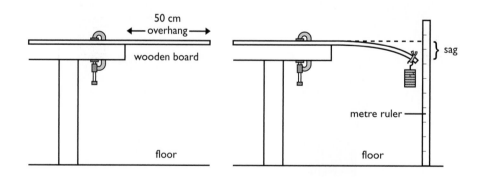

(a) (i) Explain why their teacher thought that the board would sag or break. (2)

(ii) The boys found that the board sagged by 1 cm even without any mass added to it. Why did this happen? (1)

(b) One part of the layout had a crane for adding boxes to trucks. The crane is shown in the diagram below.

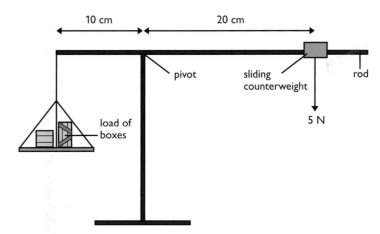

(i) Calculate the turning moment produced by the counterweight about the pivot when the crane arm is balanced horizontally. (2)

(ii) Calculate the weight of the boxes. Show your working. (2)

(iii) Billy noticed that the loading crane did not always turn freely. Name one **substance** he could add to the pivot to help with this problem, and **explain** why it would work. (2)

23.6 Two pupils wanted to investigate friction between steel and other materials. They used the apparatus shown in the diagram below.

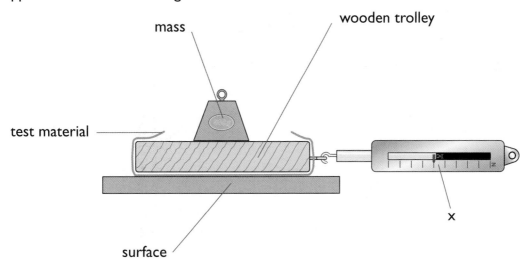

(a) (i) What is the name of the apparatus labelled X? (1)

(ii) Explain why it might be necessary to add the mass to the trolley. (1)

(b) In this investigation, what would be

(i) the **input** (independent) **variable**? (1)

(ii) the **outcome** (dependent) **variable**? (1)

(iii) two **fixed** (controlled) **variables**? (2)

(iv) Why should the pupils take three readings for each material? (1)

(c) The pupils obtained the following results:

material	test 1 (N)	test 2 (N)	test 3 (N)
P	2.0	2.0	2.0
Q	4.5	4.4	4.6
R	3.0	3.3	3.4
S	1.1	1.0	0.9
T	6.3	6.7	6.5

(i) Calculate the mean values for each of the materials. Give your answers to 1 decimal place. (2)

(ii) Which material would be best for the soles of a rock climber's boots? (1)

(iii) Which material would be best to rub onto the blades of a pair of ice skates? (1)

(iv) What do you think would happen to the values for material R if the pupils polished the surface before they carried out the investigation? (1)

23.7 The diagram below shows a crane lifting a load. The crane has a movable counterweight.

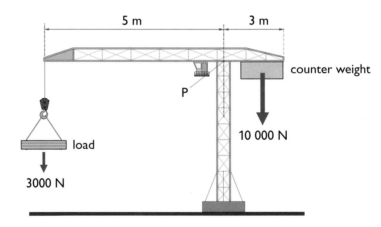

(a) Why does the crane need a counterweight? (1)

(b) (i) What would be the turning moment of a 3000 N load about the pivot at P? (1)

(ii) If the crane is balanced when a 4500 N load is being lifted, what moment must the 10 000 N force have? (1)

(iii) How far from the pivot should the counterweight be placed? (1)

(iv) What is the maximum load the crane should lift? (1)

24: Light

24.1 Which option best completes each of the following sentences? (10)

(a) An example of a reflector and not a luminous source is

the Sun	the Moon
a motorbike's headlights	a Bunsen burner flame

(b) A material which does not allow light to pass through it is

solid	opaque
transparent	a shadow

(c) Compared with a Formula 1 racing car, light travels

more slowly	at about the same speed
much more quickly	slightly more quickly

(d) The light sensitive region of the eye is the

retina	eyeball
lens	screen

(e) The image observed in a plane mirror is not

upright	the same size as the object
back to front	in front of the mirror

(f) When light is reflected from a plane mirror, the angle of

incidence is greater than the angle of reflection
reflection is greater than the angle of incidence
incidence is equal to the angle of reflection
incidence is less than the angle of reflection

(g) The bouncing of light rays from a surface is

dispersion	refraction
reflection	diffraction

(h) The primary colours are

red, orange and green	red, blue and white
yellow, blue and green	red, blue and green

(i) The splitting of light by a prism is

dispersion	refraction
reflection	diffraction

(j) A blue filter

reflects blue light	transmits white light
transmits blue light	absorbs blue light

24.2 Sally had bought a new, red top to wear to a party. Written in white across the front of the top were the words PARTY GIRL. When she arrived at the party, the hostess had turned on a red spotlight.

(a) (i) What colour did the writing appear to be? (1)

(ii) Explain your answer. (1)

(b) The red spotlight was switched off and replaced with a blue spotlight.

(i)   What colour did the writing appear to be? (1)

(ii) What colour did the top she was wearing appear to be? (1)

(iii) Explain your answers to (i) and (ii). (1)

24.3 Two mirrors held at 90° to each other always reflect a ray of light parallel to the incident ray.

(a) In this diagram, a ray of light strikes mirror A at an angle of 45°. Copy the diagram and then use a ruler and protractor to complete the diagram to show how the mirrors reflect the ray. (2)

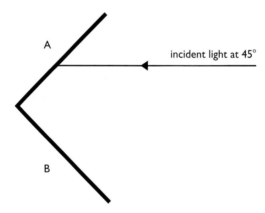

(b) In this diagram the source of light has been moved so that the ray of light strikes mirror A at a different angle. Copy the diagram and then use a ruler and protractor to complete the diagram to show how the mirrors reflect the ray. (3)

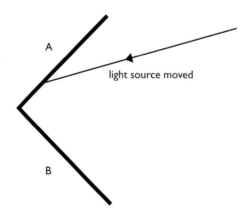

(c) Policemen, ambulance workers and firefighters wear reflective jackets when working. The relective stripes on the jackets are made up as shown in the diagram below:

reflective stripe . . .

. . . is made of small spheres of reflective substance

(i) At night, road users can see these reflective jackets in the beam of their headlights. Explain why. (2)

(ii) Why would a plane mirror not be suitable for a reflective jacket? (1)

(iii) Explain why the cloth trousers of a firefighter (which do not have reflective stripes) do not give a clear reflection. (1)

24.4 When a beam of white light is shone through a prism the beam is deflected and splits into the colours of the spectrum.

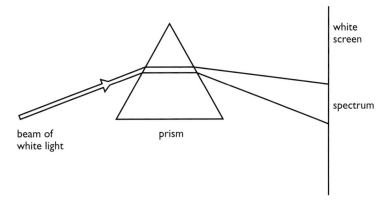

white screen

spectrum

beam of white light

prism

(a) What is the name given to the deflection of the beam by the prism? (1)

(b) What is the name given to the splitting of the white light into the colours of the spectrum? (1)

(c) The wing cases of a dead ladybird beetle were ground up in alcohol and the solid parts filtered out. This left a bright red solution. A clear container of this solution was placed between the prism and the screen.

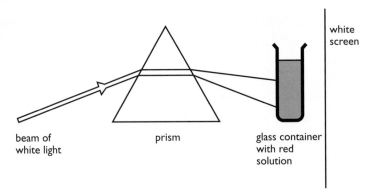

(i)   What change would you see on the screen? (1)

(ii) Explain your answer. (2)

(iii) The screen was replaced by a piece of yellow paper. What change would you see? Explain your answer. (2)

(d) Another species of beetle has a blue body with yellow stripes, and only comes out at night. A biologist was trying to study these beetles, but only had a torch with a red beam. Explain why it would be difficult to find these beetles with this torch. (2)

24.5 A snooker player is ready to play a shot, hitting the white ball against the blue. The table is well lit by a source of white light.

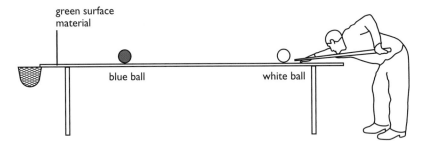

(a) Describe how light from the lamp lights up the balls and makes them visible to the player. (2)

(b) (i)   Explain why it would be difficult for the snooker player to play the shot if the white light was replaced with a red lamp. (1)

(ii) Why does the black ball look black in any light? (1)

(c) If the overhead light stops working the players might use a light source from the side of the table. Explain why this causes shadows behind the snooker balls. (1)

(d) Light from the overhead lamp shines onto the snooker balls and onto the material of the table surface. Explain how reflection from the balls is different from scattering of light by the material of the table. (2)

24.6 At a zoo, the rare Oomi bird had made a nest. The keepers at the zoo did not want to disturb the bird but wanted to allow visitors to view the nest. They built a piece of equipment like the one shown below.

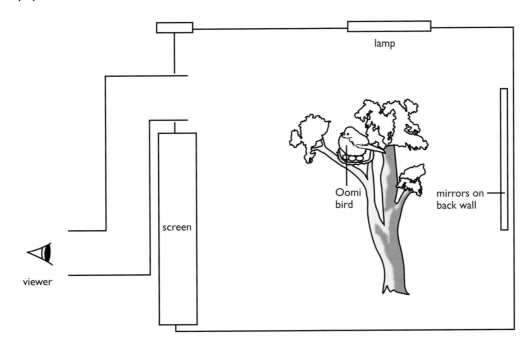

(a) Copy the diagram and add mirrors to show how the visitors would view the nest. (2)

(b) Draw a ray of light from the bird to show how it reaches the visitor's eye. Include arrows on the ray to show its direction. (1)

(c) The male Oomi bird is bright red, but the female is green. They are both sensitive to cold, and so the zookeepers use a combination lamp that gives off heat and red light.

Explain why this makes it difficult to see the female bird. (1)

(d) The zookeepers wanted to send images of the nesting birds to other parts of the zoo. They decided to use an optical fibre to do this. Copy and complete this outline diagram to explain how an optical fibre works. (3)

24.7 The diagram below shows a ray of blue light passing through a perspex block.

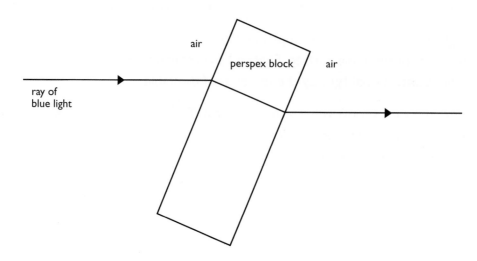

(i)   As the light goes into the block it changes direction. What is the name of this effect? (1)

(ii)   The light leaving the block is not as bright as the light entering the block. Explain why. (1)

(iii) Light can be made to pass through a prism, and to form a spectrum on a white screen.

Copy and complete this sequence to describe the colours of the spectrum. (1)

. . . . yellow . . . .

. . . . violet

25: Vibration and sound

25.1 Which option best completes each of the following sentences? (10)

(a) The sound produced by a banjo string can be made louder by

using a thinner string	plucking the string harder
shortening the string	tightening the string

(b) Compared with light, sound travels

a little more slowly	much faster
much more slowly	a little faster

(c) The first part of the human ear to vibrate when sound reaches it is the

cochlea	pinna
ear canal	eardrum

(d) Echo sounding is not used to

detect submarines	listen to a message on the phone
search for shoals of fish	locate sunken ships

(e) When an observer taps an aquarium, the speed of sound in the different parts is in the order (fastest to slowest)

glass wall – air – water – aluminium frame
aluminium frame – water – air – glass wall
air – water – aluminium frame – glass wall
glass wall – aluminium frame – water – air

(f) Permanent deafness can occur if

the pinna is infected
the nerve to the brain is damaged
the eardrum is damaged by a pressure change
the ear canal is blocked by wax

(g) Sound

travels well through space	cannot travel through air
only travels through air	cannot travel through a vacuum

(h) The size of a vibration is its

pitch	frequency
amplitude	wavelength

(i) The frequency of a sound wave is measured in

joules	hertz
millimetres	millivolts

(j) A violinist plays a note followed by one of lesser frequency. The first note will have sounded

softer	lower
louder	higher

25.2 (a) The diagrams below show the displays produced on an oscilloscope by four different sound waves

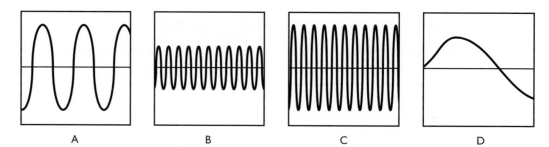

A   B   C   D

(i) Which **two** sounds have the same pitch? (1)

(ii) Which **two** sounds are as loud as one another? (1)

(b) (i) Builders using an electric drill might damage their ears. Explain how this could happen. (2)

The table below shows the maximum time that a builder can work with a drill at different sound levels without damage to his ears.

sound level (decibels)	maximum time (hours)
86	8.0
88	4.0
90	2.0
92	1.0
94	0.5
96	0.25

(ii) What is the maximum time that the builder can work when drilling into concrete and making a sound of **89** decibels? Show your working. (2)

25.3 David wanted to investigate which material would be the best sound insulator. He placed an electric bell inside a box, and then covered the box with each of the test materials in turn. The sound was detected by a sound sensor and recorded by a data logger, as shown in the diagram below.

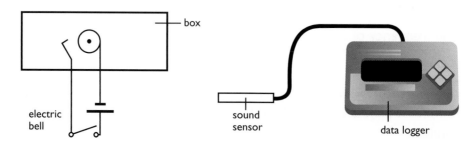

The results that David obtained are shown in the table below.

insulating material	sound level recorded
none	68
paper	60
polystyrene block	35
cardboard	54
cloth	48

(a) (i) Name the units for the sound level recorded. (1)

(ii) Draw a bar chart to represent these results. Use a graph grid like the one below. (4)

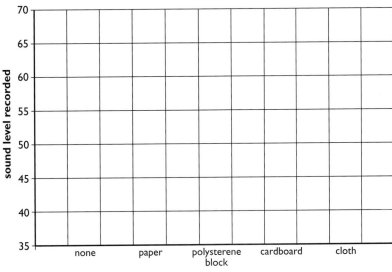

(iii) Which of the materials was the best as an insulator? (1)

(b) (i) For this investigation, name the **input** (independent) **variable**. (1)

(ii) Name the **outcome** (dependent) **variable**. (1)

(iii) Which of the following would have been **controlled variables** in his investigation? (2)

the box used
the distance between the sound sensor and the box
the person who recorded the results in the table
the light intensity in the room
the time of the day when the results were obtained

25.4 The diagram below shows part of the human ear.

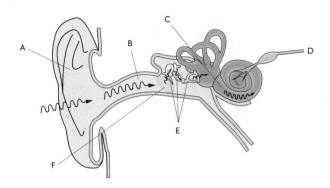

(a) Match these parts of the ear to the labels on the diagram.   (2)

eardrum	cochlea	ossicles
nerve	ear canal	pinna

(b) (i)   What happens to the eardrum when sound waves reach it?   (1)

(ii) What happens in the nerve when sound waves have had their effect on
the eardrum?   (1)

(c) The table below lists the range of frequencies that six different animals can hear.

animal	lowest frequency (Hz)	highest frequency (Hz)
human	30	20 000
robin	300	30 000
dog	30	45 000
cat	20	65 000
dolphin	80	125 000
bat	2000	110 000

(i)   A device sold by a petshop is claimed to be able to frighten cats but not to
affect birds such as robins. It does this by emitting a loud, high-pitched
sound when a cat passes in front of it. Suggest and explain a suitable
frequency for the sound emitted by the device.   (2)

(ii) Dolphins find fish to eat by releasing short bursts of high-frequency sound.
They work out how far away their prey is by measuring the time taken for
an echo of the burst of sound to come back to them.

A dolphin emits a short sound burst and hears an echo 0.2 seconds later.
Sound travels at about 1500 metres per second in salt water. Calculate
the distance of the fish from the dolphin (show your working, and include
the correct units).   (3)

25.5 The starter at the school Sports Day uses a starting gun with blank cartridges. He stands 5 m away from the starting line for each race.

(a) The starter wears ear defenders. Why does he do this? (1)

(b) Some senior pupils at the school were helping with the timing of the 200 m race. Each pupil was asked to record the time taken by a runner in a particular lane. One of them did not listen carefully to instructions, and started his stopwatch when he heard the bang from the gun and not when he saw the flash. Explain why the time he awarded to his runner would not have fitted in with the times awarded by the other pupil timers. (2)

(c) The diagram below shows where the running track was located. Some of the spectators in the seats labelled S thought that they heard two bangs at the start. Explain how this could have happened. (2)

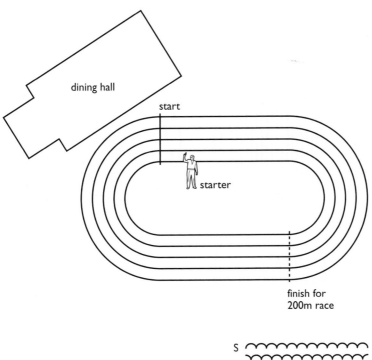

25.6 When the first astronauts landed on the Moon they were able to jump up and down, even though they wore heavy spacesuits.

(a) (i) The astronauts were able to talk to each other and to the lunar craft because they had radios rather like mobile phones in their helmets. Without the phones they could not hear each other speaking. Explain why. (1)

(ii) The astronauts were told that if their phones broke down they could talk in an emergency as long as they touched their helmets together.
Why could they hear each other when their helmets were touching? (2)

(b) (i) The astronauts were instructed to recharge their radio batteries when they returned to the spacecraft. The main batteries in the spacecraft were recharged using a freely available renewable source of energy on the Moon. Suggest what this renewable energy source is. (1)

(ii) Which energy transfer takes place in the radio battery as it is being charged? (1)

chemical to sound	sound to chemical
thermal to electrical	electrical to chemical

(c) The astronauts can tell when they are being called because they hear a buzz from the radio. The NASA technicians wanted to make sure that the buzz could be heard clearly. The diagrams below show the display on an oscilloscope for four possible sound waves.

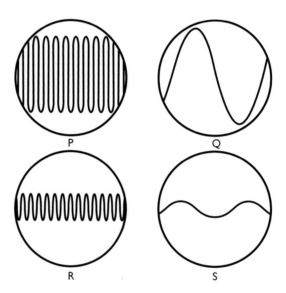

The scientists thought that a loud sound with a high pitch would be best.
Which of the oscilloscope displays matches this requirement? (1)

25.7 A teacher set up the piece of apparatus shown in this diagram.

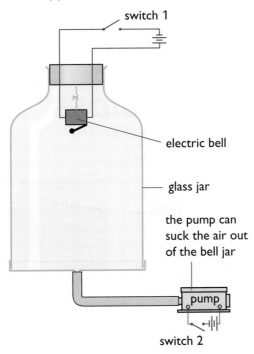

switch 1

electric bell

glass jar

the pump can
suck the air out
of the bell jar

pump

switch 2

(a) (i) Why can you hear the bell when switch 1 is closed? (1)

(ii) What can you hear when switch 2 is closed? Explain your answer. (1)

(b) Annie was not paying attention to the teacher – she was looking out of the window.
She saw two gardeners hammering in new fence posts around the hockey field.
Annie saw one of the men hit the post with a sledgehammer. One second later she
heard the sound.

(i) Why did she hear the sound after she saw the hammer hit the post? (1)

(ii) The gardener with the hammer moved halfway across the field, closer to the
science laboratory. He started to hammer on another post. How long was the
gap between Annie seeing him hit the post and her hearing the bang? (1)

| there was no gap | less than one second |
| longer than one second | exactly one second |

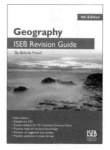